AC(

Paper P2 (INT)

Corporate Reporting

Pocket notes

KAPLAN
PUBLISHING

British library cataloguing-in-publication data

A catalogue record for this book is available from the British Library.

Published by:
Kaplan Publishing UK
Unit 2 The Business Centre
Molly Millars Lane
Wokingham
Berkshire
RG41 2QZ

ISBN 978-1-84710-801-2

© Kaplan Financial Limited, 2009

Printed and bound in Great Britain.

Contents

The exam

This exam will test your knowledge of accounting concepts, principles and theories. You will be expected to comment on scenarios and assess proposed accounting treatments.

You must be able to apply accounting theory to practical situations and will be expected to cover several accounting standards in one scenario, so you must study the breadth of the syllabus.

When providing advice on the suitability of accounting treatment you will also have to consider professional and ethical judgement.

A knowledge of current issues is also required.

The exam is three hours long with an additional 15 minutes reading time to enable candidates to read the questions and begin planning their answers. You are not allowed to write in the answer booklet during the reading time but you are allowed to write notes on the question paper.

Section A (50%) – one case study compulsory question (50 marks).

- This will be a scenario based question dealing with the preparation of consolidated financial statements including group cash flow statements and financial reporting issues.

Section B (50%) - A choice of two questions from a total of three (25 marks each).

- In this section, two questions will be scenario or case study based and one question will be an essay based on current issues. They will cover all aspects of the syllabus.

- You must ensure you revise the breadth of the syllabus, as questions are likely to cover more than one topic.

- Marks will be awarded for professional style and format of reports.

Keys to Success in Paper P2

Exercising judgement / technique

- On the compulsory question, make sure you have a thorough knowledge of all aspects of group accounting. Use your groups technique to work through the question methodically, focusing on the parts you can do. Don't panic if there are adjustments that you do not know what to do with, better to leave them and get on with the rest of the question, rather than get bogged down. Don't spend too long on the consolidation as you still have to complete the rest of the question. In the Pilot Paper, there were 35 marks available for the group cash flow and another 15 marks for written elements of the paper. Make sure you attempt all parts of this question.

- Make sure you write a report where a report is asked for – the Examiner has said this will attract presentation marks..

- Keep up to date with current issues. Aside from the possibility of having one question that covers a single new standard or exposure draft, you may also come across an issue in a scenario type question that requires you to comment on a current proposal.

- Try and step back from question scenarios and think of all of the possible impacts. It is unlikely the Examiner will give you a scenario where only one accounting standard should be applied. It is more likely to be two or three so you must recognise this and produce a valid argument for your proposed accounting treatment. Try and think of the following questions as pointers to start thinking about your answer:

What has happened in the scenario?	Comment on the issue in question, e.g. a company has entered into a share based payment transaction
What are the current accounting rules?	Current standard? Not covered by any standard?
What are the new accounting rules?	New standard? Exposure draft / Discussion paper in issue?
Apply the rules to the question scenario:	Comment on the accounting treatment that should be followed, applying the rules to the given scenario
What are the implications?	Comment on the effect of the rules discussed on the financial statements, e.g. income statement, financial position, cash flow, statement of changes in equity.
Conclude:	A one line summary of the points made above

Exam focus

- Read around the subject (Student Accountant, ACCA website, IASB website, accountancy journals) and 'A students guide to IFRS' by Clare Finch.

- Practice past exam questions; the majority of the old 3.6 questions are still relevant for P2.

- Don't forget report formats (header, introduction, headings, main body developing each point, conclusion)

- Spend an equal amount of time on each question in the exam

- Leave out the parts you cannot do – there will be things in the exam you have never seen before, if you don't know what to do, don't waste time on them.

1

Group accounting 1

In this chapter

- Definitions.
- Overview.
- Basic workings.
- Associates and joint ventures.
- Fair value adjustments.
- Other adjustments.

Overview

- There will always be a group accounting question as Q1 on this paper

- Basic principles will enable you to get the easy marks in the question before attempting any of the trickier parts.

A parent is an entity that has one or more subsidiaries.

A **subsidiary** is an entity, including an unincorporated entity, such as a partnership, that is controlled by another entity (known as the parent).

Control is the power to govern the financial and operating policies of an entity so as to obtain benefits from its activities

Non-controlling interest is the equity in a subsidiary not attributable to a parent.

Basic workings

SOFP - basic workings - overview

Group statement of financial position – standard 5 workings

Regardless of the difficulty of the question, having a process to work through will help you tackle a group accounting question.

Set out your workings as follows:

W1 Group structure

W2 Net assets of each subsidiary

	At acquisition	At statement of financial position date	Post Acquisition
	$000	$000	$000
Share capital	X	X	
Share premium	X	X	
Reserves	X	X	X
Fair value adjustments	X/(X)	X/(X)	X/(X)
	X (to W3)	X (to W4)	X (to W5)

W3 Goodwill – proportion of net assets method

	$000
Cost of investment	X
Less group share of net assets at acquisition (W2)	(X)
	———
Goodwill on acquisition – parents share	X
Less impairment to date	(X)
	———
Goodwill to consolidated statement of financial position	X

Or (dependent on accounting policy)
W3 Goodwill – fair value (full goodwill) method

	$000	$000
Cost of investment		X
Less group share of net assets at acquisition (W2)		(X)
		———
Goodwill – parents share		X
FV of NCI at acq	X	
NCI in net assets at acq	(X)	
	———	
NCI share of goodwill		X
		———
Full goodwill at acquisition		X
Less impairment		
Group share	(X)	
NCI share	(X)	
Goodwill to SOFP		X
		———

W4 Non-controlling interest – proportionate share method

	$000
NCI share of net assets at reporting date (W2)	X
Less unrealised profit in inventory (if any)	(X)
NCI to consolidated statement of financial position	X

(W4) Non-controlling interest – Fair value method

	$000
NCI x net assets at reporting date	X
NCI Goodwill (W3)	X
Less NCI% unrealised profit in inventory (if any)	(X)
Less NCI impairment of goodwill	(X)
NCI to SOFP	X

W5 Group retained earnings

	$000
Parent company (100%)	X
Subsidiary: Group share of post acquisition profit (W2)	X
Less goodwill impairment (W3)	(X)
Less group share of unrealised profit (if any)	(X)
Total group profits	X

KAPLAN PUBLISHIN

Group income statement – workings

SOCI - basic workings - overview

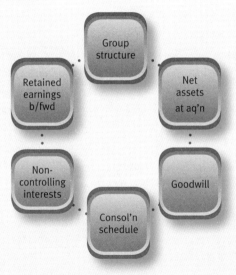

W1 Group structure (as before)

W2 Net assets at acquisition to be able to calculate goodwill (as before)

W3 Goodwill – so you can calculate the impairment charge (as before)

W4 Consolidation schedule

If the subsidiary has been acquired part way through the year, you will have to time apportion income and expenses. It is worth setting this out in a consolidation schedule working if you have time in the exam. All items from revenue down to profit after tax must be time apportioned.

	Parent	x/12 months only Subsidiary	Adjustments	Consolidated
	$000	$000	$000	$000
Revenue	X	X	(X)	X
↓				
Profit after tax	X	X	(X)	X

W5 Non-Controlling Interest

MI share of subsidiary profit after tax (must be time apportioned if a mid year acquisition)

	$000
	X

W6 Group retained earnings brought forward

	$000
Parent (100% of reserves at beginning of year)	X
Subsidiary: group share of post acquisition reserves at beginning of year	X
Less goodwill impairment at beginning of year	(X)
	X

If the subsidiary has been acquired during the year, then there will be no post acquisition reserves brought forward as the subsidiary did not belong to the group at that date.

Associates and joint ventures

Definition

- An **associate** is an entity over which the investor has significant influence and which is neither a subsidiary nor a joint venture of the associate.

- **Significant influence** is the power to participate in the financial and operating policy decisions of an entity. A holding of 20% or more of the voting power is presumed to give significant influence.

- A **joint venture** is a contractual arrangement whereby two or more parties undertake an economic activity that is subject to joint control.

Accounting for associates

Associates are not consolidated as the parent does not have control. Instead they are equity accounted.

Statement of financial position

Investment in Associate

	$000
Cost	X
Add: share of increase in net assets	X
Less: impairment losses	(X)
	X

You will need to produce W2 to calculate the post acquisition profits. In the group retained earnings (W5), the group's share of A's post acquisition profits must be included.

Income statement

Include the group's share of the Associate's **profit after tax less any impairment losses**.

Intercompany transactions

Remember that you do not eliminate intercompany sales and purchases, receivables or payables between the group and the associate as the associate is outside of the group. The only exception to this is any unrealised profit on transactions, of which the group's share must be eliminated.

Accounting for joint ventures

IAS 31 identifies three basic types of joint venture.

- **Jointly controlled operations** – involves the use of assets and resources of the venturers rather than establishing a separate entity.

- **Jointly controlled assets** – the venturers jointly control an asset dedicated to be used within the joint venture rather than establishing a separate entity.

- **Jointly controlled entities** – this involves the establishment of a separate entity in which each venturer has an interest.

Jointly controlled operations

It is rare for a jointly controlled operation to have its own financial statements. The individual financial statements of each individual venturer will recognise:

- the assets that it controls and the liabilities that it incurs

- the expenses that it incurs and its share of the revenue that it earns from the sale of goods or services by the joint venture.

Jointly controlled assets

It is unlikely that there is a full set of accounts for this type of joint venture so the individual venturers will set up a joint venture account in their own records for the income and expenses incurred in respect of the joint venture and a memorandum income statement is prepared periodically to calculate the amount payable to or receivable from the other venturers.

Jointly controlled entities

A jointly controlled entity keeps its own accounting records.

In the individual financial statements of the venturers, the investment in the joint venture is recorded at cost. In the consolidated financial statements, IAS 31 gives a choice of treatment:

- **Proportionate consolidation** – the venturer includes its share of the assets, liabilities, income and expenses of the jointly controlled entity.

- Equity method – as used for associates (IAS 28).

Fair value adjustments

IFRS 3 Business Combinations

IFRS 3 requires that on acquisition both the cost of investment and the net assets acquired are recorded at their fair value. Assets and liabilities must be recognised if they are separately identifiable and can be reliably measured. The future intentions of the acquirer must not be taken into account when calculating fair values.

 Definition

Fair value is the amount for which an asset could be exchanged, or a liability settled, between knowledgeable, willing parties in an arm's length transaction.

Rules for recognising fair values

Type of asset / liability	Fair value
Tangible non-current assets	(a) land and buildings - market value (b) plant and equipment – market value or if not available, depreciated replacement cost.
Intangible assets	Recognise at market value if there is an active market or estimated value if not (see IAS 38). **Fair value**

Type of asset / liability	
Inventory and work-in-progress	Finished goods – the selling price less the cost of disposal and a reasonable profit allowance
	Work in progress – the selling price of finished goods less costs to complete, the cost of disposal and a reasonable profit allowance
	Raw materials – current replacement cost
Quoted investments	Quoted investments should be valued at market price.

Type of asset / liability	Fair value
Contingencies	Contingent assets and liabilities should be measured at fair values where these can be determined (reasonable estimates of the expected outcome may be used).
Pensions and other post retirement benefits	The fair value of a deficit or surplus in a pension or other post retirement benefits scheme should be recognised as a liability or an asset of the acquiring group.
Deferred tax	Deferred tax on adjustments to record assets and liabilities at their fair values should be recognised in accordance with the requirements of IAS 12 Income taxes.

Fair value of the cost of acquisition

The cost of acquisition is:

(a) the amount of cash paid; plus

(b) the fair value of other purchase consideration given by the acquirer; plus

(c) Include contingent consideration even if it is not deemed to be probable of payment at the date of acquisition.

Note:

- If payment of cash is deferred it should be discounted to present value using a rate at which the acquirer could obtain similar borrowing.

- If the acquirer issues shares, fair value is normally the market price at the date of acquisition.

Negative goodwill

If the net assets acquired exceed the fair value of consideration, then negative goodwill arises.

After checking that the calculations have been done correctly, negative goodwill is credited to the income statement immediately.

Other adjustments

Don't forget that there are other adjustments that you may be required to make. These have been seen in previous studies and include:

- dividends paid by the subsidiary or associate and wrongly accounted for by the parent

- interest on intercompany loans that has not been accounted for by the receiving party

- intercompany management charges that have not been accounted for by the receiving party

- intercompany sales, purchases and unrealised profit in inventory

- intercompany transfer of non-current assets and unrealised profit on transfer

- intercompany receivables, payables and loans that need eliminating.

Exam focus

You are likely to encounter fair value adjustments, and accounting for associates and joint ventures in many group accounts questions. They will form the basis of many questions which include additional group accounting, and other, requirements.

Within EN-gage Complete Text Chapter 1, attempt TYU 6 H, S & A.

Recent past exam questions in this area include:

- Pilot Paper – Zambeze Group part (b)
- December 2007 – Beth
- June 2008 – Sirus
- December 2008 - Marrgrett.

Group accounting 2

In this chapter

- Overview.
- Vertical groups.
- D Shaped / mixed groups.
- Step by step.
- Disposal of subsidiaries.

Overview

Exam focus

- These more complex situations are likely to feature in every exam as part of the compulsory Q1.

- They are technically challenging but with the approach in the previous chapter and key points illustrated below, you should be able to attempt the questions with confidence.

Vertical groups

- A vertical group arises when a parent company has a subsidiary which has investments of it own.

- If the parent controls the subsidiary, it will also control the subsidiary's investments.

- Determine the group status by looking at the control relationship.

- Watch dates carefully, to check when the sub-subsidiary became part of the group.

- Use effective interest for ownership, e.g. goodwill, NCI, group retained earnings.

Example: A acquired 75% of B on 1 January 20X7 after B had acquired 60% of C on 1 January 20X4.

What is the group structure and when does C become a member of the A group?

Solution

A
|
75%
|
B
|
60%
|
C

C becomes a member of the A group at the later of the two dates of acquisition – i.e. from 1 January 20X7.

The effective group interest in C is:

75% x 60% = 45%.

The effective NCI in C is 55%

D Shaped / mixed groups

- Similar to a vertical group but the parent also has a direct investment in the sub subsidiary.

- Determine group status by looking at the control relationship.

- Use effective interest for ownership, e.g. goodwill, non-controlling interest, group retained earnings.

All consolidation workings are the same as those used in vertical group situations, with the exception of goodwill.

The goodwill calculation for the sub-subsidiary differs in that two elements to cost must be considered.

- The cost of the parent's direct holding.

- The parent's percentage of the cost of the subsidiary's holding (the indirect holding).

Example

Example: X acquired 60% of Y in 20X1 and 24% of Z in 20X2. Y acquired 35% of Z in 20X1.

What is the group structure and when does Z become a member of the X group?

Solution:

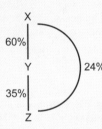

Z becomes a member of the X group once X has access to control most of the equity shares in Z – i.e. from 20X2.

The effective group interest in Z is:

24% + (60% x 35%) = 45%.

The effective NCI in Z is 55%

By the time X acquired Y, Y already held the investment in Z so the date of acquisition for both Y and Z was 20X1 and Z would be an associate. One year on, X bought enough of the shares to enable control of Z with 59% controlled by the X group. From then on, Z would be a subsidiary.

Step by step

This is a situation where a subsidiary or associate is acquired in stages, often called a step by step acquisition. There is more than one date of acquisition.

Example

A bought 10% of B on 1 Jan 20X3, a further 20% on 1 Jan 20X4 and lastly 35% on 1 Jan 20X5. What is the status of the investment? How will it be accounted for?

Solution

1 Jan 20X3   Simple investment (investment at cost in SOFP, dividend income in income statement).

1 Jan 20X4   Associate (equity accounted)

1 Jan 20X5   Subsidiary (consolidated)

If any equity interest is subsequently increased and control achieved:

(i) re-measure the previously held equity interest to fair value on the date control is achieved

(ii) recognise any resulting gain or loss in profit or loss

(iii) calculate goodwill

Disposal of subsidiaries

Key Point

- Disposals are only ever an issue for the income statement

- The statement of financial position shows the position at the year end after the disposal has occurred

- Where control is lost the profit or loss on disposal must be calculated, both in the parent's individual accounts as well as the group accounts

- In the income statement, consolidate the subsidiary up to the date of disposal and then either equity account if associate status remains, include dividend income if a simple investment remains or do nothing if a full disposal has occurred

- Where control is not lost no gain or loss on disposal is calculated and the difference between the proceeds received and the change in the non-controlling interest is accounted for in equity.

Group profit on disposal:

Sale proceeds		X
Add: Fair value of any residual holding		X
Net assets of subsidiary at disposal date:		
Share capital	X	
Retained earnings	X	
	X	
Carrying value of unimpaired goodwill	X	
	X	
Less: NCI at disposal date:		
NCI share of unimpaired goodwill (if on fair value basis)	(X)	
NCI share of net assets	(X)	
		(X)
		X

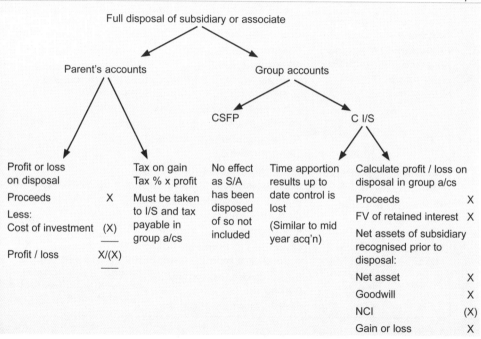

Full disposal of subsidiary or associate

Parent's accounts

Group accounts

CSFP

C I/S

Profit or loss on disposal

Proceeds	X
Less:	
Cost of investment	(X)
Profit / loss	X/(X)

Tax on gain

Tax % x profit

Must be taken to I/S and tax payable in group a/cs

No effect as S/A has been disposed of so not included

Time apportion results up to date control is lost

(Similar to mid year acq'n)

Calculate profit / loss on disposal in group a/cs

Proceeds	X
FV of retained interest	X
Net assets of subsidiary recognised prior to disposal:	
Net asset	X
Goodwill	X
NCI	(X)
Gain or loss	X

Status before disposal	Status after disposal	Treatment in consolidated income statement	Treatment in consolidated statement of financial position
Subsidiary (e.g.80%)	Subsidiary (e.g.60%)	Consolidate for the whole period. Calculate NCI to reflect change of shareholding. 20% × profit up to disposal (time apportion results) 40% × profit after disposal (time apportion results)	Consolidate as normal. Non-controlling interest is based on year-end shareholding.
Subsidiary (e.g.80%)	Associate (e.g.40%)	Consolidate up to date of disposal (time apportion results). Equity account post disposal (time apportion results). Include group gain on disposal.	Equity account based on year-end shareholding.
Subsidiary (e.g.80%)	Simple investment (e.g.10%)	Consolidate up to date of disposal (time apportion results). Include dividend income post disposal Include group gain on disposal.	Recognise the holding retained as an investment, measured at fair value at the date of disposal

Mid year disposals: treatment of dividends

The disposed of subsidiary may have paid, declared or proposed a dividend in the year of disposal and when the disposal is mid year, this dividend may impact the calculation of net assets at disposal date.

- If the dividend has been paid prior to disposal, then the seller will have received the amount of the dividend attributable to the shares disposed of and the net assets of the subsidiary will have been reduced by the cash payment. Make sure that the full amount paid is deducted from the net assets at the date of disposal.

- If the dividend has been declared prior to disposal, then shares will be sold ex-div and the relevant amount of this dividend belongs to the seller. The net assets of the subsidiary must be reduced by the liability. Again, make sure that the full amount is deducted from the net assets at the date of disposal.

- If the dividend has been declared or proposed after the date of disposal, the shares will have been sold cum-div and the dividend belongs to the buyer. So no adjustment to net assets at the date of disposal is required.

Subsidiaries acquired exclusively with a view to subsequent disposal

- a subsidiary acquired exclusively with a view to resale is not exempt from consolidation.

- But if it meets the criteria in IFRS 5:

  - it is presented in the financial statements as a disposal group classified as held for sale. This is achieved by amalgamating all its assets into one line item and all its liabilities into another

  - it is measured, both on acquisition and at subsequent reporting dates, at fair value less costs to sell (IFRS

sets down a special rule for such subsidiaries, requiring the deduction of costs to sell. Normally, it requires acquired assets and liabilities to be measured at fair value).

- The criteria include the requirements that

  - the subsidiary is available for immediate sale

  - it is likely to be disposed of within one year of the date of its acquisition

  - the sale is highly probable.

- A newly acquired subsidiary which meets these held for sale criteria automatically meets the criteria for being presented as a discontinued operation.

Exam focus

Within EN-gage Complete Text Chapter 2, attempt TYU 4 Major and Tom.

Within EN-gage Complete Text Chapter 3, attempt TYU 7 Cagney & Lacey.

You are likely to encounter a range of possible examination topics from within this chapter, including:

Vertical groups

- June 2007 - Glove

Step acquisitions

- December 2007 - Beth

Disposal of subsidiaries

- December 2005 - Lateral
- December 2008 - Marrgrett.

Foreign currency

In this chapter

- Overview.
- Functional and presentation currencies.
- Individual transactions in foreign currency.
- Foreign subsidiaries.
- Hyperinflation.

Overview

- This chapter deals with foreign currency transactions as well as consolidation of foreign subsidiaries.

- Make sure you study this carefully as there are a number of rules to remember.

IAS 21 The effects of changes in foreign exchange rates provides the accounting guidance on foreign currency transactions. Its main points are detailed below.

Functional and presentation currencies

A company must determine both its functional and presentation currency.

Definition

- Functional currency is the currency of the primary economic environment where the entity operates.

- Presentation currency is the currency in which the entity presents its financial statements.

Once determined, functional currency should not be changed.

Presentation currency can be any currency and can be different from functional currency. This is particularly the case if the company is foreign-owned as the presentation currency may be that of the parent. If the presentation currency is different from the functional currency, then the financial statements must be translated into the presentation currency.

Individual transactions in foreign currency

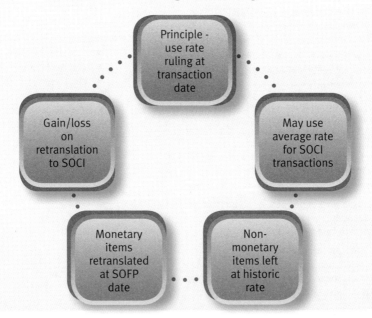

Principle - use rate ruling at transaction date

May use average rate for SOCI transactions

Non-monetary items left at historic rate

Monetary items retranslated at SOFP date

Gain/loss on retranslation to SOCI

Foreign subsidiaries

If a company has foreign subsidiaries whose functional currency is their local currency, their financial statements must be translated into the parent's presentation currency.

Key Point

- All **assets and liabilities** are translated into the parent's presentation currency at the **closing rate** at the statement of financial position.

- **Goodwill** is treated as an asset of the subsidiary and is also translated at the **closing rate**.

- **Income and expenses** in the income statement must be translated at the **average rate** for the period.

- **Exchange differences** arising on consolidation are recognised in reserves until disposal of the subsidiary when they are transferred to the income statement.

- Exchange differences arise from:

  - the retranslation of the opening net assets using the the closing rate

  - retranslation of the the profit for the year from the average rate (used in the income statement) to the closing rate (for inclusion in the statement of financial position)

  - the retranslation of goodwill at each reporting date to the closing rate.

- In an exam question the calculation of the exchange gains and losses is by far the most difficult aspect.

- In past papers this has been worth very few marks.

- The best plan is to ignore it and gain the marks elsewhere.

Set out your workings in columns as follows:

Subsidiary results €	Adjustments €	Revised results €	Rate closing rate	Subsidiary results for consolidation $

Steps:

1 Make any adjustments to the subsidiary's accounts in the foreign currency.

2 Translate the subsidiary's financial statements – statement of financial position at closing rate and income statement at average rate.

3 Do the consolidation workings as normal.

4 Prepare the consolidated income statement and statement of financial position – don't forget the adjustment for the gain or loss on the parent's investment in the subsidiary.

Since IAS 21 requires the cost of investment within the goodwill calculation to be based on the closing rate, an extra adjustment is required as part of the consolidation process.

The cost of investment held in the parent's accounts (recorded at the historic rate) must be retranslated to the closing rate. Any exchange gain or loss is taken to group reserves.

Disposal of overseas subsidiaries

On disposal of a subsidiary that has been translated into presentational currency, the cumulative exchange differences that have previously been recognised in reserves become realised. The foreign exchange reserve is taken to the income statement on the disposal of the subsidiary as part of the gain or loss on disposal. This is called recycling of gains and losses.

Equity accounting

The principles to be used in translating a subsidiary's financial statements also apply to the translation of an associate's.

Once the results are translated, the carrying amount of the associate (cost (at the closing rate) plus the share of post acquisition retained earnings) can be calculated together with the group's share of the profits for the period and included in the group financial statements.

Hyperinflation

Definition

Hyperinflation is a very high rate of inflation.

Key Point

- Hyperinflation is deemed to exist when the cumulative inflation rate over three years is approaching or exceeds 100%.

- Such high inflation renders financial information useless unless it is expressed in terms of current prices.

- Therefore, IAS 29 requires that non monetary assets (inventory, investments and non-current assets) and income and expenses are restated by applying the change in the general price index from the date of the transaction to the balance sheet date. (If a general price index is not available then use an estimate based on the exchange rate movements between the functional currency and a stable currency.)

- Monetary assets and liabilities are not restated as they are already expressed in terms of amounts owed or owing at the balance sheet date.

- Corresponding figures must also be restated to improve comparability.

Exam focus

Within EN-gage Complete Text Chapter 5, attempt TYU 4 Saint & Albans.

Foreign currency may be tested either as a group accounting question, or as part of a multi-topic question as follows:

- June 2004 - Memo
- December 2006 - Mission
- June 2008 – Ribby, Hall and Zian

4

Group statement of cash flows

In this chapter

- Overview.
- Format of the statement of cash flows.
- Dividends from associates.
- Dividends paid to non-controlling interest.
- Acquisitions and disposals.
- Foreign currency.

Overview

Key Point

- A statement of cash flows enables users of the financial statements to assess the **liquidity**, **solvency** and **financial adaptability** of a business.

- New topics to deal with in group cash flows are dividends from associates, dividends to NCI and acquisitions and disposals.

Definition

- **Cash consists of** cash in hand and deposits repayable upon demand less overdrafts. This includes cash held in a foreign currency.

- **Cash equivalents** are short term, highly liquid investments that are readily convertible to known amounts of cash and are subject to an insignificant risk of changes in value.

- **Cash flows** are inflows and outflows of cash and cash equivalents.

Exam focus

- If required to prepare a statement of cashflows, you will be producing a group cash flow as individual company cash flows have been covered in earlier papers.

- The examiner may ask you to correct a cash flow rather than prepare from first principles. Be ready for this!

Format of the statement of cash flows

IAS 7 Statement of cash flow does not prescribe a format for the cash flow statement, it requires that it is split into three sections – operating, investing and financing.

DEF Group statement of cash flows for the year ended 31 December 20X6

	$000	$000
Cash flows from operating activities		
Profit before tax	X	
Adjustments for:		
Depreciation charge	X	
Amortisation of goodwill	X	
Profit on sale of non-current assets	(X)	
Interest received	(X)	
Interest paid	X	
Operating profit before working capital changes	X	
Increase in inventories	(X)	
Increase in receivables	(X)	
Increase in payables	X	
Cash generated from operations		X
Interest paid		(X)
Income tax paid		(X)
Net cash inflow from operating activities		X
Cash flows from investing activities		
Dividends received from associate	X	
Interest received	X	
Purchase of property, plant and equipment	(X)	
Proceeds from sale of property	X	
Acquisition of subsidiary, net of cash acquired	(X)	
Net cash used in investing activities		(X)

Cash flows from financing activities

Issue of ordinary share capital	X	
Repurchase of loan	(X)	
Dividends paid to minority interest	(X)	
Dividends paid to parent shareholders	(X)	
Net cash used in financing activities		(X)
Net increase in cash and cash equivalents		X
Cash and cash equivalents brought forward		X
Cash and cash equivalents carried forward		X

Dividends from associates

In the cash flow statement we need to report the actual cash received by the group from the associate in the period. To find this, we reconcile the opening to closing balance of the investment in associate.

Dividends Paid to Non-controlling interests

When a subsidiary that is not wholly owned pays dividends, some of the cash leaves the group as the dividend paid to the minority interest. This must be shown in the group cash flow statement. The working is very similar to that for the associate (above). The non-controlling interest is reconciled from opening to closing balance and the cash paid is the balancing figure.

As with the associate, watch out for dividends payable that mean all of the cash has not been paid to the NCI. You will need to adjust the cash paid for the effect of this.

Acquisitions and disposals

If a subsidiary joins or leaves a group during a financial year, the cash flows of the group should include the cash flows of that subsidiary for the period the results of the subsidiary are included in the income statement.

The treatment of an acquisition or disposal of a subsidiary is not difficult. As seen in the proforma, the acquisition or disposal is included in investing activities. The figure shown is the net figure of two items.

- The cash spent on the purchase or received on the sale of the subsidiary.
- The cash balances (or overdraft). acquired or disposed of with a subsidiary (found in the net assets of the subsidiary at acquisition or disposal).

These two figures can be picked up very quickly from the question paper.

However, when dealing with the other balances in the cash flow, you must take out the effect of the acquisition. So, when dealing with any of the assets and liabilities in the cash flow, make sure you take out the effect of the assets or liabilities on acquisition or disposal.

Foreign currency

Foreign currency gains and losses are not cash flows so must not be included in the statement of cash flows. They will be seen as a reconciling item when trying to establish cash movements for items such as non-current assets, inventories, receivables, payables in the same way we have just seen above.

Exam focus

Within EN-gage Complete Text Chapter 6, attempt TYU 4 Boardres.

Ensure that you are familiar with the standard workings and adjustments required for group statements of cash flow.

Recent examination questions include:

- Pilot Paper – Zambeze Group
- December 2008 – Warrburt Group.

Group reorganisations and restructuring

In this chapter

- Overview.
- Reasons for reorganisations.
- Creation of new parent company.
- Changes of ownership within a group.
- Reverse Acquisitions.

Overview

- The key is to learn the rules of how to deal with a restructuring and then apply them to the question scenario.

- You must know how to deal with the different options as past questions have asked for comments on up to three restructuring plans.

Definition

A group reconstruction is any of the following.

- Transfer of ownership of a subsidiary from one group entity to another.

- Addition of a new parent entity for a group.

- Transfer of ownership of a subsidiary to a new entity which is not a group entity but has the same shareholders as the group's parent.

- The combination into a group of two or more entities whose shareholders are the same before the combination.

- The acquisition of shares of another entity which then issues shares so that the acquired entity has control of the combined entity.

Reasons for re-organisations

There are a number of reasons why a group may wish to reorganise.

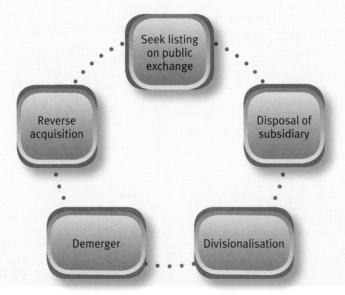

Changes of ownership within a group

Changes of ownership within a group should not affect the consolidated accounts as no assets leave or are added to the group.

Subsidiary moved up

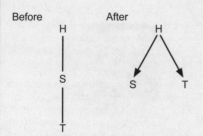

This is usually dealt with by S paying a dividend in specie of the investment in T to H. Note that in some jurisdictions it is illegal for a parent to issue shares to a subsidiary so this reorganisation cannot be carried out by a share for share exchange.

Accounting entries

S: Dr Retained earnings CR Investment in T

T: DR Investment in T CR Retained earnings

Subsidiary moved down

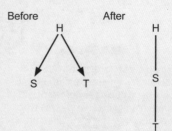

This transaction can occur in one of two ways:

1. S issues share to H in exchange for the shares in T.

2. S pays cash to H for T. H may end up with a gain on disposal which must be eliminated in the group accounts.

Subsidiary moved along

Before   After

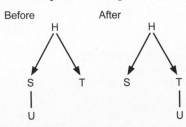

T would pay cash (or assets) to S. Consideration cannot be in shares as T may become a subsidiary or associate of S and retain an interest in U. This type of reorganisation may be done if the group wishes to sell S, but retain U.

Accounting entries:

In T's books:	Dr Investment in U
	Cr Cash
In S's books	Dr Cash
	Cr Investment in U

Reverse acquisitions

Definition

A reverse acquisition occurs when an entity obtains ownership of the shares of another entity, which in turn issues sufficient shares so that the acquired entity has control of the combined entity.

Reverse acquisitions are a method of allowing unlisted companies to obtain a stock exchange quotation by taking over a smaller listed company.

A private entity may arrange to be acquired by a listed entity. The public entity issues shares to the private entity so that the private entity's shareholders end up controlling the listed entity. Legally, the public entity is the parent, but the substance of the transaction is that the private entity has acquired the listed entity.

Group reorganisations and restructuring were retained in the current P2 syllabus. It was rarely examined under the previous syllabus and has not been examined to date under the current syllabus.

The professional and ethical duty of the accountant

In this chapter

- Overview.
- Ethical issues facing the accountant.
- Ethical codes of conduct.
- Consequences of unethical behaviour.

Overview

- **Ethics** are an important part of working as an accountant.

- Ethics is likely to come up as part of the compulsory question, as in the Pilot paper.

- You may be asked to comment on a particular situation and whether the directors have acted in an ethical manner

Ethical issues facing the accountant

Professional ethics are the principles and standards that underlie the responsibilities and conduct of a person in performing his/her function in a particular field of expertise

- Ethical principles are important in a business organisation as they set the tone for the culture and behaviour of employees and management.

- The application of ethics can sometimes be intangible. Ethics is often described as 'doing the right thing' but this can mean different things to different individuals.

Advising on corporate reporting

- An audit is an independent examination of and report on the financial statements and therefore it is expected that the auditors are independent.

- There has always been an area of contention in the accountancy profession as to whether auditors can actually be independent when their clients pay for their services.

- Another independence issue is that accountancy firms complete non-audit work for their clients in addition to the audit. This work is often of a higher value than the audit and, again, makes it

KAPLAN PUBLISHIN

difficult for the auditor to be completely independent as they potentially could lose a great deal of fee income.

- Accountancy bodies such as the ACCA issue codes of conduct and ethical guidelines that they require their members to comply with.

Preparation of accounting information

- Preparers of financial information must prepare that information honestly and fairly. Financial information may be relied upon by users of the financial statements, investors and potential investors, banks, and suppliers, so it is important that it is not misleading.

- One of the issues in preparing financial information is the pressure that may be put on individuals by officers of the organisation who are acting unethically. If an individual's manager is asking him her to prepare financial information in a misleading way, then it can be very difficult to speak up and refuse to do what is being asked for.

- Ethical codes of conduct offer guidance on how to deal with ethical issues.

Ethical codes of conduct

Professional accountants are bound by their Institute or Association's codes of ethics and are expected to act in accordance with such codes of conduct.

ACCA Code of Ethics

The ACCA Code of Ethics and Conduct applies to all students, associates and members. The Code is in the form of a framework and adopts a principles-based approach; whilst some specific rules are included, compliance is largely concerned with the observation of the fundamental principles.

- **Professional competence and due care** - Members have a continuing duty to maintain professional knowledge and skill at a level required to ensure that a client or employer receives competent professional service based on current developments in practice, legislation and techniques. Members should act diligently and in accordance with applicable technical and professional standards when providing professional services.

- **Confidentiality** - Members should respect the confidentiality of information acquired as a result of professional and business relationships and should not disclose any such information to third parties without proper and specific authority or unless there is a legal or professional right or duty to disclose. Confidential information acquired as a result of professional and business relationships should not be used for the

- **Integrity** - Members should be straightforward and honest in all professional and business relationships.

- **Objectivity** - Members should not allow bias, conflicts of interest or undue influence of others to override professional or business judgements.

personal advantage of members or third parties.

- **Professional behaviour** – Members should comply with relevant laws and regulations and should avoid any action that discredits the profession.

Consequences of unethical behaviour

Exam focus

Within EN-gage Complete Text Chapter 7, attempt TYU 1 Enron.

This will typically be examined within the compulsory question within section A of the examination. The key to gaining good marks is to apply ethical and professional principles to the scenario within the question; there will be few marks for simple repetition of ethical principles without application and explanation relevant to the specifics of the question. Recent exam questions include:

- Pilot Paper – Zambeze Group part (c)
- June 2008 – Ribby, Hall and Zian
- December 2008 – Warrburt Group part (c).

The financial reporting framework and performance reporting

In this chapter

- Overview.
- International accounting standards committee.
- IASB'S Framework.
- IAS 1 Presentation of financial statements.
- IAS 8 Accounting policies, changes in accounting estimates and errors.

Overview

- This chapter gives useful background information to the regulatory environment

- The Framework for the preparation and presentation of financial statements is very examinable, in whole or in parts

International accounting standards committee

Key Point

- The IASC Foundation is an independent not for profit foundation based in the US whose trustees appoint the members of the IASB, SAC and IFRIC.

- The IASB is responsible for developing and issuing new accounting standards.

- The SAC advises the IASB on decisions the IASB may be considering.

- The IFRIC draw up IFRIC Interpretations if a new problem arises or give guidance on the application of a standard where unsatisfactory interpretations exist.

IASB'S framework

The IASB's **Framework for the preparation and presentation of financial statements** identifies the principles on which accounting standards are to be developed. It aims to assist in the preparation of financial statements, development of new standards and to reduce alternative accounting treatments.

Key Point

- The underlying assumptions of financial statements are that they are prepared on a going concern basis and follow the accruals concept.

- Characteristics of useful financial information:

    - Relevant

    - Reliable

    - Comparable

    - Understandable.

- Financial statements should present fairly the financial performance and position of an entity. The Framework does not define fair presentation but compliance with International standards and the Framework should help to achieve this.

- Definition of elements of financial statements:

    Asset: a resource controlled by an entity as a result of past events and from which future economic benefits are expected to flow to the entity.

    Liability: a present obligation of the entity arising from past events, the settlement of which is expected to result in an outflow from the entity of resources embodying economic benefits.

    Equity is the residual interest in an entity's assets after deducting all its liabilities.

    Income is the increase in economic benefits during an accounting period.

    Expenses are decreases in economic benefits during an accounting period.

- **Recognition** of items in the financial statements

Recognition of an item in the financial statements occurs if:

- the item meets the definition of an element of financial statements,

- it is probable that any future economic benefit associated with the item will flow to or from the entity

- it can be measured at a monetary amount with sufficient reliability.

Exam focus

You will find the Framework useful in an exam as often scenarios are given which are not covered by a standard. Go back to the definitions of assets and liabilities to determine whether the transaction results in elements which meet the definitions and should be recognised.

IAS 1 presentation of financial statements

IAS 1 provides standard formats for the income statement, statement of financial position and statement of changes in equity.

Accounting concepts to apply in preparation of financial statements

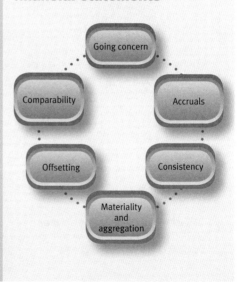

Going concern

Comparability

Accruals

Offsetting

Consistency

Materiality and aggregation

IAS 8 accounting policies, changes in accounting estimates and errors

Selecting accounting policies

Accounting policies must be determined by applying the relevant IFRS. If there is no standard, then management should choose an accounting policy that results in relevant and reliable financial information.

Changing accounting policies

Accounting policies can only change if:

- the change is required by a standard or interpretation; or

- the change results in more relevant and reliable information.

Changes in accounting policies are accounted for retrospectively as if the new policy had always been applied.

Don't confuse a change in accounting policy with a change in estimation technique. For example, depreciation is an estimation technique so the change in method should not be accounted for as a prior period adjustment.

Errors

Prior period errors are omissions from and misstatements in the financial statements arising from mistakes in applying accounting policies, oversights and the effect of fraud. They are corrected retrospectively in the first set of financial statements authorised for issue after their discovery.

Exam focus

Within EN-gage Complete Text Chapter 8, attempt TYU 1 Elements of financial statements.

You should ensure that you understand definitions from the Framework so that they can be explained and applied to information in a given scenario. Recent examination questions include:

- December 2007 – Q4 – conceptual framework
- December 2008 – Q4 – costs and benefits of accounting standards.

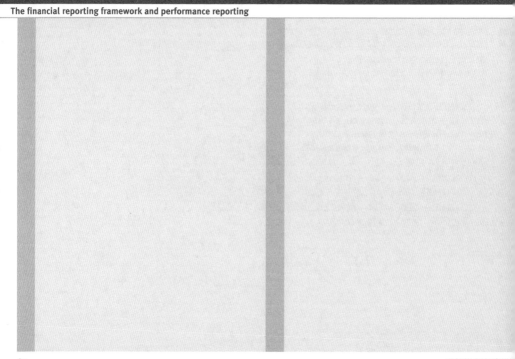

Employee benefits and share based payment

In this chapter

- Overview.
- IAS 19 Employee benefits.
- IFRS 2 Share based payment.

Overview

- Pension schemes are an important area that is examined frequently.

- You are not likely to get a full question on this topic but may find it features as part of a discussion question.

- In the past, the Examiner has included some form of pension calculation in Q1 (groups).

- You must be prepared to deal with computational and discussion elements.

Employee benefits

Background

Types of pension plan

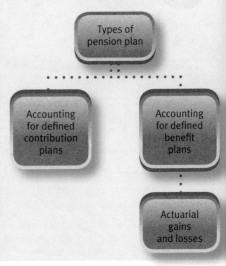

A DP was issued in March 2008 – this was the first step in a comprehensive project to review all aspects of post –employment benefit accounting, and focuses on short-term improvements to IAS 19. Essentially, any changes in the value of scheme assets and liabilities should be recognised in the period in which they occur. In the longer term, the IASB and FASB intend to work towards a new common standard on the topic.

- **IAS 19 Employee benefits** deals with accounting for pensions in the employer's accounts.

- The accounting issues lie with defined benefit schemes where an employer guarantees that an employee will have a specific pension on retirement, usually a percentage of final salary.

- To estimate the fund required, an actuary will have to calculate the contributions required to ensure the scheme has

enough funds to pay out its liabilities.

- This involves estimating what may happen in the future, such as the age profile of employees, retirement age etc.

- A pension scheme consists of a pool of assets (cash, investments, shares etc) and a liability for pensions owed to employees when they are at retirement age. The assets are used to pay out the pensions.

Measurement of pension assets and liabilities

IAS 19 requires that

- **assets** are measured at their **fair value** at the end of the reporting period date

- **liabilities** are measured on an actuarial basis and are **discounted** to present value to reflect the time value of money.

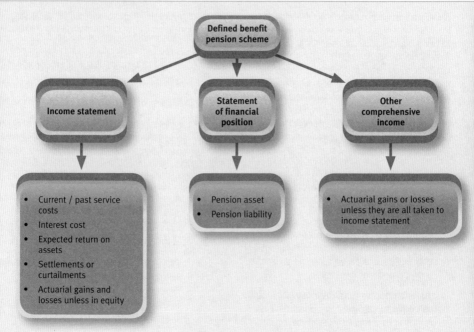

Defined benefit pension scheme

Income statement

- Current / past service costs
- Interest cost
- Expected return on assets
- Settlements or curtailments
- Actuarial gains and losses unless in equity

Statement of financial position

- Pension asset
- Pension liability

Other comprehensive income

- Actuarial gains or losses unless they are all taken to income statement

64

Explanation of terms used

Current service cost – the increase in the actuarial liability arising from employee service in the current period.

Past service cost – the increase in the actuarial liability relating to employee service in previous periods but only arising in the current period - usually due to an improvement in retirement benefits being provided.

Interest cost – the increase in the pension liability arising from the unwinding of the discount as the liability is one period closer to being settled.

Expected return on assets – the expected return earned from the pension scheme assets.

Settlements or curtailments – the gains or losses arising when employees transfer out of the pension scheme.

Actuarial gains or losses – increases or decreases in the pension asset or liability that occur due to the assumptions of the actuary being different to what actually happened, e.g. the investment income on the assets was greater than expected.

Treatment of actuarial gains and losses

As detailed above, actuarial gains and losses arise because the actuarial assumptions will not have been wholly correct. IAS 19 allows a choice of how to deal with these gains and losses.

1   If the net cumulative unrecognised actuarial gains and losses at the end of the previous period exceed the greater of 10% of the present value of the pension liability or 10% of the fair value of the plan assets, then a portion of the actuarial gains or losses must be recognised as income or expenses immediately. The portion recognised is the excess divided by the expected

average remaining working lives of the employees. . If the actuarial gains or losses do not meet the 10% corridor they do not need to be recognised, although the entity may choose to do so.

2 Another method may be used, providing that:

(a) the alternative method results in faster recognition of actuarial gains and losses

(b) the same basis is used for gains and losses

(c) the basis is applied consistently.

Hence, IAS 19 allows the UK approach which recognises actuarial gains and losses in full, in the statement of changes in equity.

Current issue

A DP was issued in March 2008 – this was the first step in a comprehensive project to review all aspects of post – employment benefit accounting, and focuses on short-term improvements to IAS 19. Essentially, any changes in the value of scheme assets and liabilities should be recognised in the period in which they occur. In the longer term, the IASB and FASB intend to work towards a new common standard on the topic.

IFRS 2 share based payments

A **share based payment** transaction is one where an entity obtains goods or services from other parties with payment taking the form of shares or share options issued by the entity.

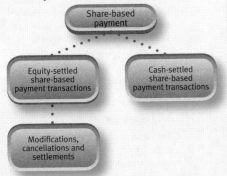

There are two types of share based payment transactions:

1 **equity-settled** share based payment transactions where a company receives goods or services in exchange for equity instruments (e.g. shares or share options).

2 **cash-settled** share based payment transactions, where a company receives goods and services in exchange for a cash amount paid based on its share price.

Accounting - general

- IFRS 2 requires that all share-based payments are recognised in the accounts.

- When a share-based payment is entered into, the goods and services received and corresponding increase in equity should be measured at fair value.

Accounting for equity settled share-based payments

- If a company issues share options (e.g. to employees) the fair value of the option at the grant date should be used as the cost of the services received.

- At each reporting date, the estimated number of share options expected to vest is then used as the basis for measurement of the equity reserve, with the expense spread over the vesting period.

- The increase in the equity reserve for the year is recognised as an expense as follows:

  - Dr Remuneration expenses
  - Cr Equity reserve

- At the vesting date, other performance conditions (e.g. minimum share price) are taken into account to establish whether the options can actually vest.

- If the options are exercised, the equity reserve is used to increase share capital and share premium as follows:

  - Dr Cash (option exercise price received)
  - Dr Equity reserve
  - Cr Share capital
  - Cr Share premium

- If the options do not vest, or are not exercised for any reason, the equity reserve remains unchanged.

How fair value of equity settled share-based payments is determined:

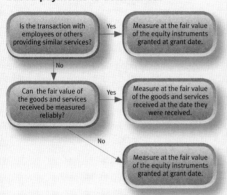

Accounting for cash settled share-based payments

- If a company grants share appreciation rights ("SARS") (e.g.to employees) the fair value of the SARS at the reporting date should be used as the cost of the services received.

- At each reporting date, the estimated number of SARS expected to vest is then used as the basis for measurement of the liability, with the expense spread over the vesting period.

- The increase in the liability for the year is recognised as an expense as follows:

  - Dr Remuneration expenses

  - Cr Liability

- At the vesting date, other performance conditions are taken into account to establish whether the SARS can actually be paid.

Accounting for deferred tax and share-based payments

- A deferred tax asset may arise with regard to equity-settled share-based payments as there is an expense recognised in the financial statements, but usually no tax relief is granted until the options are exercised at a later date.

This is normally based on the intrinsic value of the option.

- A deferred tax asset may arise with cash-settled share-based payments as there is an expense recognised in the financial statements, but usually no tax relief is granted until the liability is settled at a later date.

Definition

Grant date: the date a share based-payment transaction is entered into.

Vesting date: the date on which the cash or equity instruments can be received by the other party to the agreement.

Exam focus

Within EN-gage Complete Text Chapter 10, attempt TYU 2 Defined benefit plan.

Within EN-gage Complete Text Chapter 11, attempt TYU 3 Bahzad.

As they are not within the F7 syllabus, both retirement benefits and share-based payment are regularly examined in sections A and B of the examination. Recent examination questions include:

Retirement benefits

- December 2007 – Macaljoy
- June 2008 - Sirus

Share-based payment

- Pilot Paper – Electron
- December 2007 – Beth
- June 2008 – Ribby, Hall and Zian.

Reporting financial performance

In this chapter

- Overview.
- Reporting the substance of transactions.
- Revenue recognition.
- IFRS 5 Non current assets held for sale and discontinued operations.
- IAS 33 Earnings per share.
- IFRS 8 Operating segments.
- IAS 24 Related party transactions.

Overview

- This is a popular topic which can be examined in a discussion question.

- Often, the examiner will give a scenario that you haven't seen before so you need to apply the principle of substance over form.

- Make sure you learn how to identify the substance so you can deal with the recognition of the transaction in the accounts.

Reporting the substance of transactions

Definition

The concept of substance over form requires that transactions should be accounted for and presented in accordance with their substance and not merely their legal form.

Businesses may enter into transactions in order to keep assets and liabilities off the statement of financial position – called off balance sheet financing. This will improve ratios such as return on capital employed and gearing.

Common features of transactions where the substance is not readily apparent:

- separation of the legal title of an item from the benefits and risks associated with it

- linking a transaction with one or more others so that the commercial effect cannot be understood without reference to the series as a whole

- inclusion in a transaction of one or more options whose terms make it highly likely that the option will be exercised.

The key step in determining the substance of any transaction is to identify whether it has given rise to new assets or liabilities of the entity, and whether it has increased or decreased the entity's existing assets or liabilities.

Examples of off balance sheet financing
Off-balance sheet financing

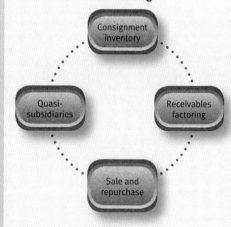

Type of transaction	Details	Substance of transaction
Consignment inventory	Inventory is held by one party but legally owned by another. E.g. a car manufacturer allows a car dealer to display cars that the dealer doesn't own. Title usually passes once the dealer sells the cars to a customer.	Determine who bears the risks and rewards of ownership as that party should record the inventory in their accounts. Usually, the substance is a loan from the manufacturer to the dealer, so the dealer must recognise the inventory, as well as a liability owing to the manufacturer.
Factoring of accounts receivable	Receivables are sold to a factor in return for a percentage of the face value of the debts. Legal title to the debts usually passes to the factor. The seller may be liable for irrecoverable debts depending on the terms of the agreement.	Determine who bears the risks and rewards of ownership of the receivables. If the seller is still responsible for irrecoverable debts then the substance is a loan from factor to seller. In this case the seller should continue to recognise the receivables as well as a liability owing to the factor.

		If the amount received by the seller is a single fixed non-returnable sum with no responsibility for irrecoverable debts, then the risk and rewards have been transferred and the receivables should be de-recognised from the SOFP.
Sale and repurchase	Assets (e.g. inventory, property) are sold to a third party with the seller having either a commitment or an option to repurchase them at some point in the future. The repurchase is usually at an increased price – reflecting interest costs.	This is a loan from the buyer to the seller. The asset should continue to be recognised on the SOFP as well as a liability owing to the buyer.
Special Purpose entities or quasi subsidiaries	Assets and liabilities are transferred to another legal entity that is not a subsidiary in order to remove them from the SOFP. E.g. A transfers a factory to B, a subsidiary of a bank in return for	If the risks and rewards of the assets and liabilities transferred are still controlled by the seller (A), then a genuine sale has not occurred. B should be recognised as a quasi subsidiary and consolidated into the accounts of A. this will show the

	cash, but continues to operate the factory.	asset and liability being kept off the statement of financial position of A. The subsidiaries set up for these transactions would only have this transaction in their accounts.

Revenue recognition

IAS 18 Revenue provides detailed guidance on accounting for revenue.

Definition

Revenue is the gross inflow of economic benefits during the period arising from the ordinary activities of the entity.

Recognition

- Revenue from the sale of goods can be recognised when the seller transfers the risks and rewards of ownership to the buyer.

- Revenue from the rendering of services is recognised by reference to the stage of completion at the balance sheet date.

- In both cases above, the amount of revenue and costs incurred must able to be measured reliably and it is probable

that economic benefits will flow to the entity as seller.

- Revenue from interest, royalties and dividends should be recognised when receipt is probable and revenues are measurable, as follows:

    - interest is recognised using the effective interest method;

    - royalties are accrued in accordance with the relevant contract;

    - dividends are recognised when the shareholders right to receive payment is established.

Measurement

- Revenue should be measured at the fair value of consideration received or receivable.

- In most cases this will be the amount agreed between the two parties as the price, adjusted for discounts if necessary.

- If the time value of money is material, then the revenue should be discounted to present value and the unwinding of the discount treated as interest income in the income statement. In this case, there are effectively two transactions –the sale of the goods and the provision of finance.

IFRS 5 non current assets held for sale and discontinued operations

Definition

A discontinued operation is a component of an entity that either has been disposed of, or is classified as held for sale; and

- represents a separate major line of business or geographical area of operations

- is part of a single coordinated plan to dispose of a separate major line of

business or geographical area of operations

- is a subsidiary acquired exclusively with a view to resale.

An entity should classify a non-current asset or a disposal group as held for sale if its carrying value will be recovered principally through a sale transaction rather than continued use in the business.

A **disposal group** is a group of assets to be disposed of, by sale or otherwise, together as a group in a single transaction, and liabilities directly associated with those assets that will be transferred in the transaction.

Assets can only be classified as held for sale (and therefore a discontinued operation) if they meet all of the criteria below:

- management commits itself to a plan to sell

- the asset (or disposal group) is available

for immediate sale in its present condition

- sale is highly probable and is expected to be completed within a year from date of classification

- the asset (or disposal group) is being actively marketed for sale at a reasonable price compared to its fair value

- it is unlikely that significant changes will be made to the plan or it will be withdrawn.

If there are events outside the entity's control that mean that the sale cannot be completed within one year and there is evidence that the entity remains committed to the plan to sell, then the asset or disposal group can still be classified as held for sale.

If the criteria are met after the balance sheet date but before the accounts are authorised for issue, the assets should not be classed as held for sale but the information should be disclosed.

Measurement

- A non-current asset (or disposal group) classified as held for sale should be measured at the lower of its carrying value and fair value less costs to sell.

- Assets classified as held for sale should not be depreciated, regardless of whether they are still in use by the reporting entity.

Presentation

Information about discontinued operations should be presented in the financial statements.

- On the face of the income statement, a single amount comprising:

- the total of the post tax profit or loss of discontinued operations

- the post tax gain or loss on the measurement to fair values less costs to sell or the disposal of the discontinued operation.

- Either on the face of or in the notes to the income statement an analysis of the single amount described into:

  - the revenue, expenses and pre tax profit or loss of discontinued operations

  - the related tax expense

  - the gain or loss recognised on the measurement to fair value less costs to sell or on the disposal of the discontinued operations

  - the related tax expense.

IAS 33 earnings per share

Exam focus

- You are unlikely to get a question which requires only the calculation of EPS.

- Questions may to focus on discussion of accounting errors and then EPS is recalculated after the profits have been adjusted.

Key Point

- Earnings per share is an important ratio that is used as a comparison for company performance and forms part of the Price / Earnings ratio.

- IAS 33 applies to all listed companies. Private companies must follow the standard if they disclose an EPS figure.

Basic earnings per share

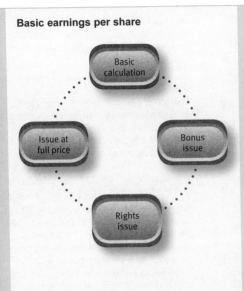

- **Basic earnings per share** is:

$$\frac{\text{profit or loss for the period attributable to the ordinary shareholders}}{\text{weighted average number of ordinary shares outstanding in the period}}$$

- Basic earnings are profit after tax less minority interest and preference dividends

- Weighted average number of ordinary shares must take into account when the shares were issued in the year.

- Partly paid shares are treated as a fraction of an ordinary share to the extent that they were entitled to participate in dividends relative to a fully paid share.

Changes in share capital

- **Issue at full market price** – as this share issue will bring cash into the business and increase earnings from the date the shares were issued, the weighted average number of shares must be calculated to ensure that the increase in earnings is matched with the increase in shares.

- **Bonus issue** – as there is no cash received; there is no effect on earnings. Therefore a bonus issue reduces EPS as share capital increases but earnings do not. The bonus issue is treated as if it has always been in issue, so share capital is adjusted at the beginning of the year and the comparative figures are adjusted for the effect of the bonus issue for comparability.

- **Rights issue** – the rights issue will bring cash into the business but not full price per share as the shares are issued below full market price. This share issue is treated as a combination of a bonus issue and a rights issue. Firstly, the bonus element must be dealt with by adjusting the opening capital by the rights issue bonus fraction:

Fair value of share before exercise of rights

Theoretical ex rights price

The theoretical ex rights price is the average price of the shares after the rights issue has taken place.

Secondly, the weighted average no of shares is calculated by time apportioning the shares according to the date of issue to match the increase in earnings with the increase in shares.

As there is a bonus element with a rights issue, the comparative must be adjusted.

Diluted earnings per share

- IAS 33 requires diluted earnings per share to be disclosed as well as basic EPS

- Diluted EPS shows the effect on the current EPS if all the potential ordinary shares had been issued under the greatest possible dilution.

- Potential ordinary shares consist of:

  - convertible loan stock

  - convertible preference shares

  - share warrants and options

  - partly paid shares

  - rights granted under employee share schemes

  - rights to ordinary shares that are conditional.

- The profit used in the basic EPS calculation is adjusted for any expenses that would no longer be paid if the convertible instrument was converted into shares, e.g. preference dividends, loan interest.

- The weighted average number of shares used in the basic EPS calculation is adjusted for the conversion of the potential ordinary shares. This deemed

Disclosure of EPS

- **Basic and diluted** earnings per share for continuing operations should be presented on the face of the income statement for each class of ordinary share.

- **Basic and diluted** earnings per share for **discontinued operations** should be presented on the face of the income statement or in the notes to the accounts for each class of ordinary share.

- If a company discloses an EPS using a different earnings figure, the alternative calculation must show basic and diluted EPS with equal prominence. These **alternative calculations** must be presented in the notes to the financial statements, not on the face of the income statement.

IFRS 8 operating segments

IFRS 8 Operating segments requires an entity to disclose information about each of its operating segments.

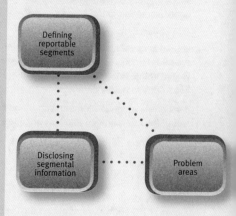

Definition

An **operating segment** is a component of an entity:

- that engages in business activities from which it may earn revenues and incur expenses;

- whose operating results are regularly reviewed by the entity's chief operating decision maker to make decisions about resources to be allocated to the segment and assess its performance; and

- for which discrete financial information is available.

A **reportable segment is** an operating segment that is used in an entity's internal management reports. Therefore management identifies the operating segments

Reporting thresholds

An entity must separately report information about an operating segment that meets any of the following quantitative thresholds:

- its reported revenue, including both sales to external customers and inter segment sales, is 10 per cent or more of the combined revenue of all operating segments.

- its reported profit or loss is 10 per cent or more of the greater, in absolute amount, of

- the combined reported profit of all operating segments that did not report a loss and

- the combined reported loss of all operating segments that reported a loss.

- Its assets are 10 per cent or more of the combined assets of all operating segments.

At least 75% of the entity's external revenue should be included in reportable segments. So if the quantitative test results segmental disclosure of less than this 75%, other segments should be identified as reportable segments until this 75% is reached.

Disclosures

IFRS 8 requires detailed disclosures, including:

- factors used to identify the entity's reportable segments, including the basis of organisation (for example, whether segments are based on products and services, geographical areas or a combination of these).

- the types of products and services from which each reportable segment derives its revenues.

For each reportable segment an entity should report:

- a measure of profit or loss

- a measure of total assets

- a measure of total liabilities (if such an amount is regularly used in decision making).

Problem areas with IFRS 8:

- Segments are defined by the directors
- Common costs – how are they allocated?
- Segment operating results may be distorted by trading with other segments on non-commercial terms
- There is no definition of segment results and segment assets within IFRS 8

IAS 24 related party disclosures

- Related party transactions are important as without disclosure they can affect the true and fair view of financial statements

- This is important if one company has subordinated its interests because of a related party relationship.

- In the exam you may have to determine related party relationships and transactions.

- Make sure you know the definition of related parties as well as the disclosure requirements.

Definition

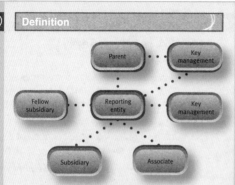

A party is related to an entity if:

(a) directly or indirectly through one or more intermediaries, the party

    (i) **controls**, is controlled by, or is under common control with the entity

    (ii) has an interest in the entity that gives it **significant influence** over the entity

    (iii) has **joint control** over the entity.

(b) the party is an **associate** of the entity (as defined in IAS 28 Associates)

(c) the party is a **joint venture** in which the entity is a venturer

(d) the party is a member of the **key management personnel** of the entity or its parent

(e) the party is a **close member of the family** of any individual referred to in (a) or (d)

(f) the party is an entity that is controlled, jointly controlled or significantly influenced by, or for which significant voting power in such an entity resides with, directly or indirectly, any individual referred to in (d) or (e)

(g) the party is a post-employment benefit plan for the benefit of employees of the entity, or of any entity that is a related party of the entity.

Definition

A **related party transaction** is the transfer of resources, services or obligations between related parties regardless of whether a price is charged.

Disclosures

- Relationships between parents and subsidiaries irrespective of whether there have been transactions between the parties.

- The name of the parent and the ultimate controlling party (if different).

- Key management personnel compensation in total and for each short term employee benefits, post employment benefits, other long term benefits, termination benefits and share based payment.

- For related party transactions that have occurred, the nature of the relationship and detail of the transactions and outstanding balances.

- The disclosure should be made for each category of related parties ((a) to (g) above) and include:

  (a) the amount of the transactions

  (b) the amount of outstanding balances and their terms

  (c) allowances for doubtful debts relating to the outstanding balances

  (d) the expense recognised in the period in respect of irrecoverable or doubtful debts due from related parties.

Exam focus

This chapter includes segment reporting and related parties, both of which are outside of the F7 syllabus and therefore highly examinable at paper P2. Ensure that you understand the definitions which apply to both segment reporting and related parties so that you can apply them to the information within a given scenario.

Within EN-gage Complete Text Chapter 9, attempt TYU 1 Revenue recognition.

Within EN-gage Complete Text Chapter 12, attempt TYU 1 Segment information.

Within EN-gage Complete Text Chapter 13, attempt TYU 1 X Ltd.

Recent examination questions include:

Reporting financial performance

*   December 2007 – Ghorse

Substance of transactions

*   December 2008 - Johan

Segment reporting

*   June 2004 - Enterprise
*   June 2008 – Norman

Related parties

*   June 2004 – Enterprise
*   June 2006 - Egin.

Non-current assets

In this chapter

- Overview.
- IAS 16 Property, plant and equipment.
- IAS 40 Investment property.
- IAS 38 Intangible assets.
- IAS 36 Impairment of assets.
- IAS 20 Accounting for government grants and disclosure of government assistance.

Overview

- This chapter focuses on standards relating to tangible and intangible assets.

- All of these have been studied previously but are regularly examined.

- This chapter is a reminder of the key points.

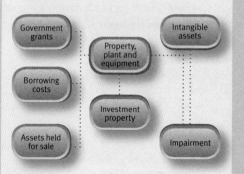

IAS 16 property, plant and equipment

- An important standard that should be learnt as any element is examinable.

Key Point

- An asset's cost is its purchase price, less any trade discounts or rebates, plus any further costs directly attributable to bringing it into working condition for its intended use.

- **IAS 23 Borrowing costs** (revised 2007) requires **finance costs** to be capitalised providing they are directly attributable to the asset being constructed. Capitalisation commences when construction expenditure is being incurred and ceases when the asset is ready for use.

- **Subsequent expenditure** on non-current assets may be capitalised if it:

  - enhances the economic benefits of the asset e.g. adding an new wing to a building

  - replaces part of an asset that has been separately depreciated and has been fully depreciated; e.g. furnace that requires new linings periodically

  - replaces economic benefits previously consumed, e.g. a major inspection of aircraft.

- The aim of **depreciation** is to spread the cost of the asset over its life in the business.

- The **depreciation method** and **useful life** of an asset should be reviewed at the end of each year and revised where necessary in accordance with IAS 8. This is not a change in accounting policy.

- If an asset has parts with **different lives**, (e.g. a building with a flat roof), the component parts of the asset should be capitalised and depreciated separately. It is not acceptable to provide for the cost of replacing the asset.

Revaluation of tangible non-current assets

- Revaluation of non-current assets is **optional**.

- If one asset is revalued, all assets in that class must be revalued, i.e. no cherry-picking.

- Where an entity adopts a policy of revaluation it need not be applied to all classes of tangible non-current assets held by the entity

- Valuations should be kept up to date to ensure that the carrying amount does not differ materially from the fair value at each reporting date.

- Revaluation **gains** are credited to the revaluation reserve in equity unless the gain reverses a previous revaluation loss of the same asset previously recognised in the income statement.

- Revaluation **losses** are debited to the income statement unless the loss relates to a previous revaluation surplus, in which case the decrease should be debited to the revaluation reserve to the extent of any credit balance existing in the revaluation reserve relating to that asset.

Accounting for revaluations

Steps:

(1) Restate asset from cost to valuation.	Dr Non-current asset cost (valuation – cost)
(2) Remove any existing depreciation provision.	Dr Accumulated depreciation
(3) Include increase in carrying value in (valuation revaluation reserve.	Cr Revaluation reserve – old carrying value)

Depreciation is charged on the revalued amount less residual value (if any) over the **remaining useful life** of the asset.

A **reserves transfer** of the **excess depreciation** is taken from the revaluation reserve to retained earnings annually and disclosed in the Statement of Changes in Equity.

Note that assets **held for sale** are recognised at fair value less costs to sell in accordance with IFRS 5. See previous chapter.

IAS 40 investment property

Definition

Investment property is property held to earn rentals or for capital appreciation or both, rather than for:

- use in the production or supply of goods or services or for administration purposes; or

- sale in the ordinary course of business.

Investment property is not:

- owner occupied property (deal with under IAS 16)

- property held for sale in the normal course of business (deal with under IAS 2 Inventories)

- property being constructed for third parties (deal with under IAS 11 Construction contracts)

- property being constructed or developed for future use as investment property (deal with under IAS 16 until it is complete).

Accounting treatment

- An entity can choose either the **cost model** or the **fair value model**.

- The **cost model** is the normal accounting treatment set out in IAS 16.

- The **fair value model** recognises investment properties in the statement of financial position at **fair value** (usually market value).

- **Gains** and **losses** on revaluation when using the fair value model are recognised in the **income statement**.

IAS 38 Intangible Assets

Definition

An **intangible asset** is an identifiable non-monetary asset without physical substance.

Accounting treatment

- An intangible asset is initially recognised at cost if all of the following criteria are met.

  (1) It is identifiable – it could be disposed of without disposing of the business at the same time.

  (2) It is controlled by the entity – the entity has the power to obtain economic benefits from it, for example patents and copyrights give legal rights to future economic benefits.

  (3) It will generate probable future economic benefits for the entity – this could be by a reduction in costs or increasing revenues.

  (4) The cost can be measured reliably – this is straightforward if the asset was purchased outright. If the asset was acquired in a business combination then the initial cost will be the fair value.

- If an intangible does not meet the recognition criteria, then it should be charged to the income statement as it is incurred. Items that do not meet the criteria are internally generated goodwill, brands, mastheads, publishing titles, customer lists, research, advertising, start-up costs and training.

- Intangible assets should be amortised, normally using the straight line method, over the term of their useful lives.

- If it can be demonstrated that the useful life is indefinite; no amortisation should be charged but an annual impairment review must be carried out.

- Goodwill and intangible assets can be revalued but fair values must be determined with reference to an active market. This will have homogenous products, willing buyers and seller at all times and published prices.

- The recognition of internally generated intangible assets is split into a research phase and a development phase. Costs incurred in the research phase must be charged to the income statement as they are incurred. Costs incurred in the development phase should be recognised if they meet the following criteria:

  (a) the project is technically feasible

  (b) the asset will be completed then used or sold

  (c) the entity is able to use or sell the asset

  (d) the asset will generate future economic benefits (either by internal use or there is a market for it)

  (e) the entity has adequate technical, financial and other resources to complete the project

  (f) the expenditure on the project can be reliably measured.

- Amortisation over the useful life of the new product or process will commence once the project is complete.

- Where development costs have been capitalised, and the expenditure has already been allowed for tax purposes when incurred, this will create a deferred tax liability as any subsequent amortisation will be added back to arrive at taxable profits.

IAS 36 impairment of assets

Definition

- This is a very important standard which has been frequently examined

- You need to know how to test for impairment, the indicators of impairment and the recognition of impairment losses.

Key Point

An **impairment loss** is the amount by which the carrying amount of an asset or cash-generating unit exceeds its recoverable amount.

- Impairment is measured by comparing the carrying value of an asset with its recoverable amount.

- If the carrying value exceeds the recoverable amount, the asset is impaired and must be written down.

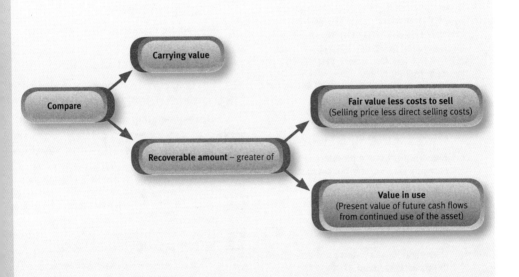

Indicators of impairment

Unless an impairment review is required by another standard (e.g. IAS 38 for intangible assets not amortised or IFRS 3 for purchased goodwill), then impairment reviews are required where there is an indicator of impairment.

Examples

Internal

- Physical damage to the asset.

- Management committed to reorganisation of the business.

- Obsolete assets.

- Idle assets.

- Major loss of key employees.

- Operating losses in the business where the assets are used.

External

- Competitor actions.

- Increasing interest rates (affects value in use).

- Market values of assets falling.

- Change in the business or market where assets are used (e.g. govt action).

Cash-generating units (CGU)

Definition

A **cash-generating unit** is the smallest identifiable group of assets that generates cash inflows that are largely independent of the cash inflows from other assets or groups of assets.

Key Point

- It will not always be possible to base the impairment review on individual assets as an individual asset may not generate a distinguishable cash flow. In this case the impairment calculation should be based on a CGU.

- The impairment calculation is done by comparing the carrying value of the CGU to the recoverable amount of the CGU. This is done by allocating an entity's assets, including goodwill, to CGUs.

- Impairment losses are allocated to assets with specific impairments first, then allocated in the following order:

  1 goodwill

  2 remaining assets on a pro rata basis.

  No asset can be written down below the higher of fair value less costs to sell, value in use and zero.

- Impairment test of goodwill in a subsidiary company – if necessary goodwill should be grossed-up to use the notional gross carrying value of the subsidiary in the impairment test. Only the group share of any goodwill impairment is accounted for in the group accounts.

- Impairment test of goodwill in a subsidiary company – if goodwill is accounted for on a fair value basis, any impairment of goodwill is allocated between the group and non-controlling interest based upon their respective shareholdings.

Recognition of impairment losses

Assets held at cost: The amount of the impairment is charged to the income statement for the period in which the impairment occurs.

Revalued assets: The impairment is charged to the revaluation reserve to reverse any previous surplus on that asset in the same way as a downward revaluation.

IAS 20 accounting for government grants and disclosure of government assistance

Definition

Government grants are transfers of resources to an entity in return for past or future compliance with certain conditions.

Accounting treatment

Grants should not be recognised until the conditions for receipt have been complied with and there is reasonable assurance that the grant will be received.

- Grants should be recognised in the income statement so as to match them with the expenditure towards which they are intended to contribute.

- Income grants given to subsidise expenditure should be matched to the related costs.

- Income grants given to help achieve a non-financial goal (such as job creation) should be matched to the costs incurred to meet that goal.

- Grants for purchases of non-current assets should be recognised over the expected useful lives of the related assets. There are two acceptable accounting policies for this:

  - deduct the grant from the cost of the asset and depreciate the net cost; or

  - treat the grant as deferred income. Release the grant to the income statement over the life of the asset. This is the method most commonly used.

Exam focus

This chapter includes accounting for property, plant and equipment, intangible assets and impairments which are likely to be examined regularly at paper P2, within both section A and B of the examination. Ensure that you understand the definitions and accounting treatments required by the reporting standards so that you can apply them to the information within a given scenario.

Within EN-gage Complete Text Chapter 14, attempt TYU 4 factory explosion.

Within EN-gage Complete Text Chapter 14, attempt TYU 8 Hyssop.

Recent examination questions include:

- Pilot paper – Electron
- December 2008 - Johan.

11

Leases

In this chapter

- IAS17 - Leases.

IAS 17

IAS 17 Leases deals with a complicated area that was frequently used to disguise liabilities on the statement of financial position. The point of IAS 17 is to identify those leases that are effectively financial instruments used to acquire the rights and benefits associated with a particular asset. These are then classified as liabilities in the statement of financial position.

Not all leases have to be treated in this way. Some leases do not give the lessee the rights and benefits of ownership (e.g. when a business hires a van for a week).

A **finance lease** is a lease that transfers substantially all the risks and rewards incidental to ownership of an asset to the lessee.

An **operating lease** is any lease other than a finance lease.

Leasing questions often ask you to explain why a particular agreement should be treated as a finance lease or an operating lease. The question will imply one or the other in terms of whether the lessee has the risks and rewards of ownership. In general, a lease is a finance lease if:

- the leased asset is likely to become the property of the lessee at the end of the agreement (either automatically or because there is an option that is likely to be exercised)

- the lease (including any secondary term that is likely to be taken up) is likely to run for most of the asset's useful life

- the present value of the minimum lease payments is close to the fair value of the asset at the commencement of the lease

- the asset is of a specialised nature that makes it particularly suited to the lessee.

This list is not intended to be exhaustive. Every question has to be approached on its own terms.

Substance over form

The treatment required by IAS 17 effectively accounts for the economic substance of finance leases rather than their legal form. The economic substance is that the lessee has borrowed an amount equivalent to the fair value of the asset and used that sum to purchase the asset itself. The fact that the lessee may never become the legal owner of the asset is ignored.

Accounting for finance leases

At the start of the lease:

- the fair value (or, if lower, the present value of the minimum lease payments) should be included as a non-current asset, subject to depreciation

- the same amount (being the obligation to pay rentals) should be included as a loan, i.e. a liability.

In practice, the fair value of the asset or its cash price will often be a sufficiently close approximation to the present value of the minimum lease payments and therefore can be used instead.

The asset is depreciated over the shorter of the asset's useful life and the term of the lease (including any secondary term that is likely to be taken up).

Each lease payment is split between:

- a repayment of the lease liability
- a finance charge.

The examiner will have to tell you how to split lease payments between capital repayments and finance charges.

Questions normally state the interest rate implicit in the lease. This makes it easy to determine the finance charges that were incurred during the period. This approach is called the "actuarial method".

If the interest rate implicit in the lease is not stated then it might be possible to derive it if the cash flows are sufficiently simple. It is just the internal rate of return of the cash flows. Alternatively, it is possible to make a crude estimate by using the "sum of the digits" method.

Example - Actuarial method

An asset with a fair value of $5,710 is leased for four years, with the option to continue the lease for a further four years at a negligible 'peppercorn' rent. The asset's useful life is nine years.

Lease payments of $2,000 are made annually at the end of every year for the first four years.

The interest rate implicit in this lease is 15%. Read the details about the cash flows very carefully. In particular, make sure that you know whether the lease payments should be deducted at the beginning of the period or the end. If the lease is to be treated as a finance lease then the asset will be capitalised at $5,710 at the start of year 1. It will be depreciated over eight years (the secondary term is likely to be taken up).

The first year's interest will be based on 15% of $5,710 = $856.

The first lease payment of $2,000 can be split $856 finance charge and $1,144 capital.

At the end of the first year, we will have a liability of $5,710 − 1,144 = $4,566.

We need to split the liability between current and non-current liabilities. We do this by determining the capital that is to be repaid in year two:

- Year two's finance charge = 15% of $4,566 = $685.
- Year two's capital repayment = $2,000 − 685 = $1,315.

At the end of year one, the total liability on the lease is $4,566, split:

- Current liabilities $1,315
- Non-current liabilities $3,251.

These figures will appear in the statement of financial position as at the end of year 1.

Year 1's income statement will show:

- Finance charge on lease $856
- Depreciation (one eighth of $5,710) $714

You should only use the sum of the digits method if the examiner does not give you sufficient information to use the actuarial method.

Interest payments for year 1
= 4/10 of $2,290 = $916

Interest payments for year 2
= 3/10 of $2,290 = $687

This means that $2,000 – 916 = $1,084 will be repaid during year 1 and $2,000 – 687 =

$1,313 will be repaid during year 2.

The asset will still be recorded at a cost of $5,710.

The statement of financial position at the end of year 1 will show a liability totalling $5,710 – 1,084 = $4,626. This can be split:

- Current liabilities $1,313
- Non-current liabilities $3,313

Year 1's income statement will show:

- Finance charge on lease $916
- Depreciation $714

Sale and leaseback transactions

- Sale and finance leaseback transactions do not transfer the risks and rewards associated with the asset. Therefore, continue to recognise the asset and depreciate as normal, with the cash receipt accounted for as receipt of a loan. The substance of the lease repayments are that, in effect, they are loan repayments which incorporate a finance charge.

- Sale and operating leaseback transactions do transfer the risks and rewards associated with the asset, which should then be derecognised upon disposal. However, the transactions may or may not be at arm's length – the following diagram illustrates the possible situations.

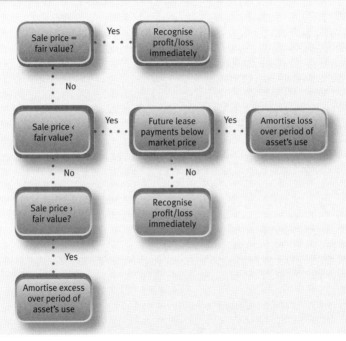

Disclosure

IAS 17 requires the following disclosures by lessees for finance leases:

- for each class of asset, the net carrying amount at the statement of financial position date
- liability for finance leases split between current liabilities and non-current liabilities
- depreciation charge in the income statement
- finance charge in the income statement.

These disclosures are necessary, partly because the leased assets are treated as the lessee's for accounting purposes, but they are not actually the lessee's property. That could be significant if, for example, a potential lender was evaluating a loan applicant's capacity to offer security for a loan.

Operating leases

Operating leases are not capitalised in the same way as finance leases.

Most operating leases will be short term in nature and the lease payments will be written off as expenses as and when they are incurred.

If an operating lease spans more than one accounting period the rental charges should be charged to the income statement on a straight-line basis over the term of the lease, unless another systematic and rational basis is more appropriate. This might arise if, for example, an office block was leased for three years while the lessee's own premises are being refurbished.

Any difference between amounts charged on operating leases and amounts paid will be treated as prepayments or accruals in the statement of financial position.

For non-cancellable operating leases with a term of more than one year, commitments should be disclosed in summary form, giving the amounts and periods in which the payments will become due.

Exam focus

Be prepared to deal with lease accounting in either section A or section B of the examination paper. In section A the requirement will be to apply the correct accounting treatment within the large consolidated accounts question. In section B the requirement may be to comment on appropriateness of accounting treatment in a given scenario. If this is the case, the accounting treatment may be wrong and this will need to be identified, explained and corrected.

Within EN-gage Complete Text Chapter 15, attempt TYU 2 Sale and leaseback transactions.

Recent examination questions in this area include:

- Pilot Paper – Electron
- December 2007 – Ghorse
- December 2008 - Johan.

Financial instruments

In this chapter

- Overview.
- Presentation of financial instruments.
- Disclosure of financial instruments.
- Measurement of financial instruments.
- Derivatives.
- Hedge accounting.

Overview

There are three accounting standards dealing with financial instruments:

- IAS 32 Financial instruments: presentation

- IAS 39 Financial instruments: recognition and measurement

- IFRS 7 Financial instruments: disclosures.

Exam focus

- This is a highly examinable area and must be reviewed in detail.

- The Examiner has published a number of articles on financial instruments as it's an area in which students make lots of errors.
  Make sure you read them.

Definition

A financial instrument is any contract that gives rise to a financial asset of one entity and a financial liability or equity instrument of another entity

Presentation of financial instruments

Classification of financial instruments

Key Point

- If a company issues a financial instrument (e.g. loans or shares) it should be classified as either **equity** or **liabilities**.

- Financial instruments must be classified according to their **substance**.

- If an **obligation** to repay cash or exchange financial instruments exists then it **must** be classified as a **liability**.

- If redeemable preference shares provide for redemption of a fixed amount or on a fixed date then they must be classified as a liability as there is an obligation to repay.

Convertible debt

- Convertible debt is debt that can be **converted into shares** on maturity rather than being redeemed for cash.

- It is debatable as to whether it is a debt or equity instrument in SOFP.

- As we have to classify financial instruments according to their substance, convertible debt has to be **split** into a **debt element** and an equity element as it consists of both.

- To split the debt into its components, calculate the present value of the capital and interest repayments using a market interest rate for debt without the conversion option. This is the debt element. Deduct this from the proceeds of issue. The balancing figure is the equity component.

Further points

- **offsetting** of financial assets and financial liabilities is **not permitted** unless there is a legal right of set off or they will be settled on a net basis

- if preference shares are classified as a liability, then the related dividend must be shown as **interest** in the income statement.

Disclosure of financial instruments

IFRS 7 requires the following disclosures:

The two main categories of disclosures required are:

1 information about the significance of financial instruments

2 information about the nature and extent of risks arising from financial instruments.

The qualitative disclosures describe:

- risk exposures for each type of financial instrument

- management's objectives, policies, and processes for managing those risks

- changes from the prior period.

The quantitative disclosures provide information about the extent to which the entity is exposed to risk, based on information provided internally to the entity's key management personnel. These disclosures include:

- summary quantitative data about exposure to each risk at the reporting date

- disclosures about credit risk, liquidity risk, and market risk as further described below

- concentrations of risk.

Measurement of financial instruments

IAS 39 Financial instruments: recognition and measurement deals with the measurement of financial instruments. This standard requires the recognition of financial instruments in the financial statements.

- IAS 39 has detailed rules on the measurement of financial instruments

- this is complex but highly examinable and must be learned.

Exam focus

Initial recognition

Financial assets and liabilities should be recognised at fair value which is usually their cost.

Subsequent measurement

For the purpose of subsequent measurement, financial instruments have to be classified into four categories and re-measured as shown below.

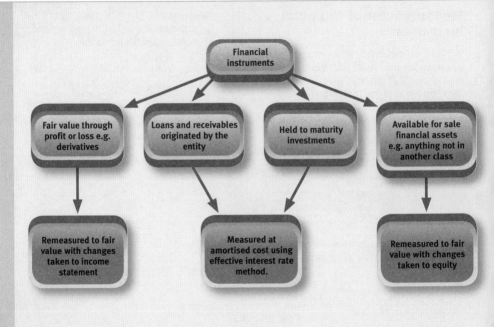

Impairment of financial assets

- At each reporting date, an assessment should be made as to whether there has been any impairment of financial assets.

- Note that for assets held at fair value, this will have been dealt with on the re-measurement to fair value.

- Impairment losses are recognised in the income statement.

Derivatives

Definition

A derivative is a financial instrument with all three of the following characteristics:

1 its value changes in response to the change in a specified interest rate, security price, commodity price, foreign exchange rate or similar variable

2 it requires little or no initial investment

3 it is settled at a future date.

Derivatives include:

- options
- forward contracts
- futures
- swaps.

As seen previously, derivatives are measured at fair value with changes recognised in the income statement. However, if a derivative is used as a hedge, then changes in value are recognised in equity.

Hedge accounting

Definition

Hedge accounting is the accounting treatment where the gains or losses on the **hedging instruments** are recognised in the same performance statement and in the same period as the offsetting gains or losses on the **hedged items**.

A hedging relationship exists when a company can define three elements.

1 A hedged item – the asset/liability or transaction on which risks need to be reduced;

2 A hedging instrument – the instrument (usually a derivative) used to offset the risks on the hedged item; and

3 The hedged risks – the specific risk (currency, interest rate etc) that is being hedged.

In order to follow the hedge accounting rules in IAS 39, the following criteria need to be met.

1 The hedge must be documented at inception and the elements of the hedging relationship defined (hedged item and instrument).

2 The hedge is expected to be highly effective.

3 The effectiveness of the hedge can be measured reliably.

4 Forecast transactions must be highly probable in order to be hedged'.

5 The effectiveness of the hedge must be able to be assessed and measured on an on-going basis.

Types of hedge

There are three types of hedge. Only two are examinable.

* Fair value hedge

* Cash flow hedge

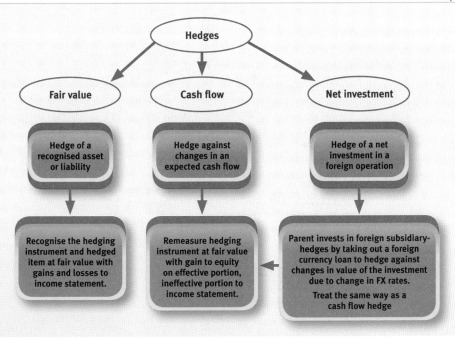

Current issues

- DP issued March 2008 with the objective of reducing complexity in reporting financial instruments.

- In March 2009, amendments to IFRS 7 were issued as a response to the global financial crisis. This introduced enhanced disclosures regarding fair value measurement and liquidity risk arising from financial instruments.

- Proposed amendments to IAS 39 designed to improve derecognition criteria, move towards convergence with US GAAP and provide relevant information to users regarding risk exposure relating to financial assets.

Exam focus

Financial instruments can appear in both sections A and B of the examination. You should understand the definitions of each class of financial asset and liability, together with their accounting treatment.

Within EN-gage Complete Text Chapter 16, attempt TYU 4 Bell.

Within EN-gage Complete Text Chapter 16, attempt TYU 7 Hoggard.

Recent exam questions in this area include:

- December 2005 – Ambush
- June 2008 - Sirus.

chapter 13

Provisions and events after the reporting period

In this chapter

- IAS 37 Provisions, contingent liabilities and contingent assets.
- IAS 10 Events after the reporting period.

IAS 37 provisions, contingent liabilities and contingent assets

Definition

- A provision is a liability of uncertain timing or amount.

- A contingent liability is a possible obligation arising from past events whose existence will only be confirmed on the occurrence of uncertain future events outside of the entity's control.

- A contingent asset is a possible asset that arises from past events and whose existence will only be confirmed on the occurrence of uncertain future events outside of the entity's control.

Provisions

Recognition

Recognise when:

- an entity has a present **obligation** (legal or constructive) as a result of a past event,

- it is **probable** that an outflow of resources embodying economic benefits will be required to settle the obligation, and

- a **reliable estimate** can be made of the amount of the obligation.

Measurement

- The amount recognised as a provision should be the **best estimate** of the expenditure required to settle the present obligation at the reporting date.

- Where the time value of money is material, the provision should be discounted to present value.

Exam focus

- In an exam question scenario, ask yourself if the expenditure can be avoided.

- If it can, there is no obligation and the provision should not be recognised.

Capitalised provisions – where there is a future obligation, for example to dismantle an installation or restore land and buildings back to their original condition, the present value of the obligation is capitalised as part of the cost of the asset as follows:

- Dr Non-current assets
- Cr Provisions

The amount capitalised is depreciated over the expected useful life of the asset. There is also an annual finance cost associated with unwinding the present value of the future obligation.

```
                    ┌─────────────────────┐
                    │  Specific guidance  │
                    └─────────────────────┘
```

Future operating losses
- Provisions should not be recognised for future operating losses.

Onerous contracts
- Provisions should be recognised for the present obligation under the contract.
- E.g. non-cancellable lease, provide for the unavoidable lease payments.

Restructuring
- Provisions can only be recognised where an entity has a constructive obligation to carry out the restructuring.
- A constructive obligation arises: when there is a detailed formal plan, identifying at least:
  - the business concerned,
  - the principal locations affected,
  - the location, function, and approximate number of employees being made redundant,
  - the expenditures that will be incurred,
  - when the plan will be implemented; and

  there is a valid expectation that the plan will be carried out by either implementing the plan or announcing it to those affected.

Contingent liabilities should not be recognised. They should be disclosed unless the possibility of a transfer of economic benefits is remote.

Contingent assets should not be recognised. If the possibility of an inflow of economic benefits is probable they should be disclosed.

IAS 10 events after the reporting period

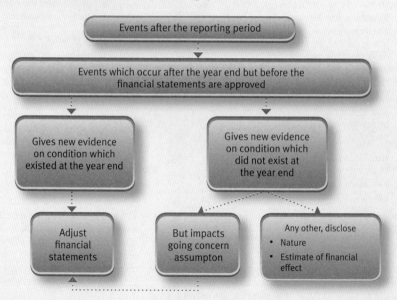

Definition

- **Events after the reporting period** are those events, favourable and unfavourable, that occur between the reporting date and the date when the financial statements are authorised for issue.

- **Adjusting events** after the reporting period are those that provide evidence of conditions that existed at the reporting period.

- **Non-adjusting events** after the end of reporting period are those that are indicative of conditions that arose after the end of reporting period.

Accounting treatment

- **Adjusting events** affect the amounts stated in the financial statements so they must be adjusted.

- **Non-adjusting** events do not concern the position at the end of reporting period

so the accounts are not adjusted. If the event is material then the nature and its financial effect must be **disclosed**.

Examples of adjusting events

- The sale of inventory after the end of reporting period which gives evidence about the inventory's net realisable value as at the reporting date.

- The bankruptcy of a customer after the reporting period confirms that a provision is required against a receivable balance at the reporting date.

- The discovery of fraud or errors that show that the financial statements are incorrect.

- The settlement after the reporting date of a court case that confirms that the entity had a present obligation at the reporting date. This would require a provision to be recognised in the financial statements (or an existing provision to be adjusted).

Examples of non-adjusting events that would require disclosure

- A major business combination after the reporting date or disposing of a major subsidiary.

- Announcing a plan to discontinue an operation.

- Major purchases and disposals of assets.

- Destruction of a major production plant by a fire after the reporting date.

- Announcing or commencing a major restructuring.

- Abnormally large changes after the reporting date in asset prices or foreign exchange rates.

Dividends

- Ordinary dividends declared **after** the reporting date are **not recognised** as liabilities at the reporting date.

- If the liability did not exist at the reporting date, then it cannot be recognised.

- This is consistent with IAS 37 and the definition of a liability in the Framework.

Provisions and events after the reporting period tend to be examined within section B of the examination. They will normally require application of definitions to the scenario or facts of the situation. They may also require judgement to identify incomplete or imprecise information provided within the question, together with correction of inappropriate accounting treatment.

Within EN-gage Complete Text Chapter 17, attempt TYU 6 Oil rig.

Within EN-gage Complete Text Chapter 17, attempt TYU 7 Events after the reporting period.

Recent examination questions include:

- Pilot Paper – Electron
- December 2007 - Macaljoy.

14

Tax in financial statements

In this chapter

- Overview.
- IAS 12 Income taxes.

Overview

Exam focus

- IAS 12 covers both current and deferred tax, but deferred tax is the most examinable and will be reviewed here.

- Past questions on deferred tax have focused on discussion of the principles.

- Make sure you know the rules of how deferred tax is provided as often this will be required.

- You must know how to do the calculations but these will only be a background to the discussion.

IAS 12 Income taxes

Definition

- Deferred tax is the estimated tax payable in future periods in respect of taxable temporary differences.

- Temporary differences are differences between the carrying amount of an asset or liability in the SOFP and its tax base.

- Tax base is the amount attributed to an asset or liability for tax purposes.

Sources of temporary differences

- Revenue accounted for on an accruals basis in the accounts, but taxed on a cash basis when received (e.ge royalties and interest received, deferred income).

- Expenses accounted for on an accruals basis in the accounts, but tax relief granted when the cash payment is made.

- Tax deductions for the cost of non-current assets that have a different pattern to the write-off in the financial statements – often referred to as accelerated capital allowances.

- Development costs that were capitalised

and amortised in the accounts, but deducted as incurred for tax purposes.

- A revaluation surplus on non-current assets will increase the accounts carrying value, without changing the tax base of the asset.

- Pension obligations that are recognised in the accounts, but only allowable for tax when the contributions are actually paid into the scheme.

- Losses in the income statement where tax relief is available only against future taxable profits.

- A deferred tax asset may arise with regard to equity-settled share-based payments as there is an expense recognised in the financial statements, but usually no tax relief is granted until the options are exercised at a later date. This is normally based on the intrinsic value of the option.

- A deferred tax asset may arise with

cash-settled share-based payments as there is an expense recognised in the financial statements, but usually no tax relief is granted until the liability is settled at a later date.

Business combinations can have several deferred tax consequences:

- The assets and liabilities of the acquired business are revalued to fair value. The revaluation to fair value of the assets does not always alter the tax base, and if this is the case, a temporary difference will arise.

- The deferred tax recognised on this difference is deducted in measuring the net assets acquired and, as a result, it increases the amount of goodwill.

- The goodwill itself does not give rise to deferred tax as IAS 12 specifically excludes it.

- The acquirer may be able to utilise the benefit of its own unused tax losses against the future taxable profit of the acquiree. In such cases, the acquirer recognises a deferred tax asset, but does not take it into account in determining the goodwill arising on the acquisition.

  - On an on-going basis, there may be intra-group profits (e.g. on inventory) that are unrealised in the group accounts, but which are taxable in the individual company accounts.

  - Unremitted earnings of group companies: a temporary difference may arise where the accounts carrying value of a subsidiary, associate or trade investment is different from the tax base. The accounts carrying value is normally based on the net assets plus goodwill, whereas the tax base will be the initial cost of the investment. Normally deferred tax should be recognised on such temporary differences, but If reversal of the temporary difference can be controlled, or it is probable that it will not reversed, then deferred tax need not be accounted for. As an associate cannot be controlled (unlike a subsidiary), deferred tax would normally be accounted for.

  - Trade investments would not normally have deferred tax implications unless they have been revalued.

Accounting treatment

- IAS 12 requires **full provision** for all taxable temporary differences (except for goodwill) using the balance sheet liability method.

- Deferred tax assets can be recognised for all deductible temporary differences to the extent it is probable that profits will be available for these differences to be utilised.

- IAS 12 does not permit the discounting of deferred tax liabilities.

- The charge for deferred tax is recognised in the income statement account unless it relates to a gain or loss that has been recognised in equity e.g. revaluations, in which case the deferred tax is also recognised in equity.

- Deferred tax should be measured at the rates expected to be in force when the temporary differences reverse, although usually the current tax rate is used.

Exam focus

The normal focus for tax-related issues in the examination is deferred tax. As part of a larger question, it can be examined in both section A and B of the examination; it can also be the main focus of a question in section B.

Within EN-gage Complete Text Chapter 19 attempt TYU 1 Temporary differences.

Recent examination questions include:

- December 2005 - Panel
- Pilot Paper – Kesare Group
- December 2007 - Ghorse.

Non financial reporting

In this chapter

- Overview.
- Sustainability reporting.
- Environmental reporting.
- Social reporting.
- Human capital management reporting.
- Management commentary.

Overview

- Questions set on this topic are likely to be a mixture of discussion or scenario based.

- Make sure that you understand the reasons behind reporting as well as the requirements for it.

Key Point

- Large businesses are accepting the idea that they are responsible to a wider group of stakeholders, rather than just their shareholders.

- There is a demand for information on the environmental and social impact of companies' activities.

- Increasingly, companies are considering the environmental and social impact of their actions when making business decisions, sometimes called **corporate citizenship**.

Stakeholders

The stakeholders of a business are as follows:

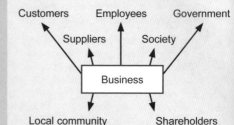

The needs of stakeholders may be different - compare shareholders with local community- but if a company considers the needs of its stakeholders, then for example, it may consider the environmental impact of its activities, provide fair remuneration to employees, and pay suppliers promptly.

Sustainability reporting

Definition

Sustainability is the process of conducting business in such a way that it enables an entity to meet its present needs without compromising the ability of future generations to meet their needs.

- In a corporate context, sustainability means that a business entity must attempt to reduce its environmental impact through more efficient use of natural resources and improving environmental practices.

- Sustainability reports include highlights of non-financial performance such as environmental, social and economic reports during the accounting period.

- There is no framework for sustainability reporting in IFRS, so this reporting is voluntary.

- However, the most accepted framework for reporting sustainability is the Global Reporting Initiative's Sustainability Reporting Guidelines which were issued in 2002.

The **Global Reporting Initiative**'s guidelines suggest a report should contain:

- a statement from the CEO describing the key elements of the report

- an overview of the organisation and scope of report

- executive summary and KPIs used

- discussion of the vision and strategy of the organisation including environmental and social performance

- overview of the governance structure including information on stakeholders

- economical, environmental and social performance, reporting use of energy, emissions, waste, transport, suppliers, products, health and safety, non discrimination, training, human rights and community development.

A number of high profile companies follow the GRI guidelines, e.g. Boots plc, Royal Dutch / Shell group plc, J Sainsbury plc, Cadbury Schweppes plc, Vodafone plc.

Environmental reporting

Definition

Environmental reporting is the disclosure of information in the published annual report or elsewhere, of the effect that the operations of the business have on the natural environment

Most environmental reports take the form of a combined statement of policy and review of activity. They cover issues such as:

*   waste management

*   pollution

*   intrusion into the landscape

*   the effect of an entity's activities upon wildlife

*   use of energy, and

*   the benefits to the environment of the entity's products and services.

Information in the financial statements

Without an environmental report, the only information seen in the annual report would be:

*   charges to the income statement for environmental costs incurred in the period, or

*   disclosure of any environmental provisions or contingencies made in accordance with IAS 37.

Environmental costs include:

- environmental measures which are the costs of preventing, reducing or repairing damage to the environment and the costs of conserving resources

- Environmental losses which are costs which bring no benefit to the business, for example:

  - fines, penalties and compensation

  - impairment or disposal losses relating to assets which have to be scrapped or abandoned because they damage the environment.

Social reporting

Definition

Corporate Social Responsibility is the continuing commitment by business to behave ethically and contribute to economic development while improving the quality of life of the workforce and their families as well as of the local community and society at large.

Contents of social reports

- The GRI guidelines include social reporting aspects.

- The Institute of Social and Ethical Accountability suggest the following should be included.

  - Information about relationships with stakeholders, e.g. employee numbers, wages and salaries, provision of facilities for customers and information about involvement with local charities.

  - Information about the accountability of the entity, e.g. sickness leave, accident rates, noise levels, numbers of disabled employees, compliance with current legal, ethical and industry standards.

– Information about dialogue with stakeholders, e.g. the way in which the entity consults with all stakeholders and provides public feedback on the stakeholders' perceptions of the entity's responsibilities to the community and its performance in meeting stakeholder needs.

Human capital management reporting

Definition

Human Capital Management (HCM) relates to the management of the recruitment, retention, training and development of employees.

If an organisation invests in its workforce to ensure that it has the right mix of skill and experience, then this should bring competitive advantage.

In the UK, the Accounting for People Taskforce was set up in January 2003 by the government. One task was to review HCM reporting. They recommend that HCM reports should:

- have a strategic focus linking HCM policies and practices, business strategy and its performance. They should include information on:

  – the size and composition of the workforce

  – retention and motivation of employees

  – the skills and competences necessary for success, and training to achieve these

  – remuneration and fair employment practices

  – leadership and succession planning

- be balanced and objective, following a process that is susceptible to review by auditors

- provide information in a form that enables comparisons over time.

Management commentary

Definition

Management commentary is information that accompanies financial statements as part of an entity's financial reporting. It explains the main trends and factors underlying the development, performance and position of the entity's business during the period covered by the financial statements. It also explains the main trends and factors that are likely to affect the entity's future development, performance and position.

IASB Discussion paper Management Commentary

The IASB published a discussion paper Management Commentary in October 2005. It was prepared by a number of representatives from national standard setters with the aim of presenting a preliminary view on this topic.

The IASB believe that high quality management commentary should:

(a) supplement and complement financial statement information

(b) provide an analysis of the entity through the eyes of management

(c) have an orientation to the future.

Management commentary should also possess the attributes that make the information useful to investors; namely: understandability, relevance, supportability, balance and comparability over time.

An entity should disclose information on:

(a) the nature of its business

(b) its objectives and strategies

(c) its key resources, risks and relationships

(d) its results and prospects

(e) its performance measures and indicators.

Exam focus

Non-financial reporting issues could be included within the narrative part of section A or within section B of the examination.

Within EN-gage Complete Text Chapter 20, attempt TYU 2 Social and environmental reporting.

Recent examination questions include:

- December 2007 – Beth.

16

Specialised entities

In this chapter

- Not for profit entities.
- Small and medium sized entities.

Not for profit entities

Definition

A **not-for-profit entity** is one that does not carry on its activities for the purposes of profit or gain to particular persons, including its owners or members; and does not distribute its profits or assets to particular persons, including its owners or members.

The main types of not-for-profit entity are:

- clubs and societies

- charities

- public sector organisations (including central government, local government and National Health Service bodies).

Objectives of not for profit entities

- The main objective of public sector organisations is to provide services to the general public. Their long term aim is normally to break even, rather than to generate a surplus.

- Most public sector organisations aim to provide value for money

- Other not-for-profit entities include charities, clubs and societies whose objective is to carry out the activities for which they were created.

Assessing performance in not for profit entities

- It can be difficult to monitor and evaluate the success of a not-for-profit organisation as the focus is not on a resultant profit as with a traditional business entity.

- The success of the organisation should be measured against the key indicators that reflect the visions and values of the organisation. The strategic plan will identify the goals and the strategies that the organisation needs to adopt to achieve these goals.

- Performance is sometimes measured in terms of efficiency, economy and effectiveness – the Three Es.

Definition

Small and medium sized entities

A small and medium sized entity (SME) is an entity that:

(1) does not have public accountability and

(2) publishes general purpose financial statements for external users.

Note that IFRS do not have size-based criteria as there is within UK company law for preparation and publication of abbreviated accounts for SME.

The problems of accounting for SMEs

- IFRSs were not specifically designed for large listed companies but their application in many countries is by large listed companies, which undertake many complex transactions, in financial instruments, for example. The main users of financial statements prepared under IFRS are the capital markets and hence it is widely viewed that IFRSs are designed for listed entities.

- Any SME that adopts IFRS must comply with all of the requirements of the accounting standards. There are a number of complex standards that are not necessarily relevant to the users of the SME's financial statements. Compliance with these brings a large reporting burden on the entity.

- The main users of small company financial statements are not normally external investors, but the tax authorities, lenders and potential lenders (often banks) and the owner/managers themselves. The recognition and measurement criteria used by large companies may not be appropriate and may even be positively unhelpful to owner/managers of small companies.

Possible solutions to SME reporting:

- Exemptions from compliance within existing IAS/IFRS (e.g. IAS 33 EPS applies to listed companies only)
- Devise a new set of reporting standards specifically for SME. It may be difficult to specify size-related criteria on an international basis for this to be applied consistently.

Draft IFRS for SMEs

In February 2007, the IASB issued an exposure draft setting out the proposed treatment of small and medium sized entities.

The aim of the IFRS is to provide a simplified, stand-alone set of accounting principles that are appropriate for smaller, non-listed companies and are based on full International Financial Reporting Standards (IFRS),

As compared with IFRS, the IFRS for SMEs:

- removes choices for accounting treatment; for example, the cost model must be used for property, plant and equipment and for investment properties

- eliminates topics that are not generally relevant to SMEs; for example lessor accounting for finance leases (not a big concession, when lessors are normally large institutions which would not be eligible for the IFRS for SMEs) and accounting in a hyperinflationary environment

- simplifies methods for recognition and measurement; for example, there are only two categories of financial assets and all development expenditure must be recognised as an expense.

Where the IFRS for SMEs does not specifically address a transaction, event, or condition, an SME is required to look to the requirements and guidance elsewhere in the IASB Standard for SMEs dealing with similar and related issues.

Failing that, the SME is required to adopt an accounting policy which results in relevant and reliable information; in doing so, it may (but is not required to) look to the requirements and guidance in IFRS dealing with similar and related issues.

In January 2009, the IASB issued an Exposure Draft - IFRS for Non-publicly Accountable entities. This was essentially a re-naming and redrafting of the ED first issued in 2007. It is likely that there will be a stand-alone IFRS applicable to smaller entities, whilst also permitting the adoption of full IFRS. The final standard is expected to be issued in mid-2009.

Exam focus

The topics within this chapter could be examined as part of a topical or current issue within section B of the exam.

Within EN-gage Complete Text Chapter 21, attempt TYU 1 SME's.

They have not been examined to date under the current examination syllabus.

17

Adoption of IFRS

In this chapter

- IFRS 1 First time adoption of IFRS.
- Implications of adoption of IFRS.
- Harmonisation of IFRS.

IFRS 1 first time adoption of IFRS

This standard sets out the procedures to be followed in adopting IFRS for the first time.

Definition

The **date of transition** is the beginning of the earliest period for which an entity presents full comparative information under IFRS in its first IFRS financial statements

Example

If an entity adopts IFRS for the first time in its 31 December 2007 financial statements and presents one year of comparative information, the transition date will be 1 January 2006.

Adoption of IFRS

- The entity should use the same accounting policies for all the periods presented; these policies should be based solely on IFRS in force at the reporting date.

- A major problem for entities preparing for the changeover is that IFRS themselves keep changing, although the IASB have said there will be no more standards to adopt until 2009.

- Entities will have to collect information enabling them to prepare statements under previous GAAP, current IFRS and any proposed new standards or amendments.

- IFRS 1 states that the opening IFRS statement of financial position must:

  - recognise all assets and liabilities required by IFRS

  - not recognise assets and liabilities not permitted by IFRS

  - reclassify all assets, liabilities and equity components in accordance with IFRS

- measure all assets and liabilities in accordance with IFRS.

Disclosures

- Entities must explain how the transition to IFRS affects their reported financial performance, financial position and cash flows. Two main disclosures are required, which reconcile equity and profits.

  - The entity's equity as reported under previous GAAP must be reconciled to the equity reported under IFRS at two dates:

    - the date of transition. This is the opening reporting date

    - the last reporting prepared under previous GAAP.

  - The last annual profit reported under previous GAAP must be reconciled to the same year's profit prepared under IFRS.

- Any material differences between the previous GAAP and the IFRS cash flows must also be explained.

IFRS 1 allows exemptions for certain items where it is considered the cost of complying would outweigh the benefit. Examples are:

- Previous business combinations do not have to be restated (e.g. if merger accounting had been applied which is not allowed under IFRS).

- Past currency translation reserves do not have to be shown separately from retained earnings.

- Convertible debt that has been repaid does not have to be split into debt and equity component.

Implications of adoption of IFRS

The transition to IFRS requires careful and timely planning. There are a number of questions that must be asked:

(a) Is there knowledge of IFRS within the entity?

(b) Are there any agreements (such as bank covenants) that are dependent on local GAAP?

(c) Will there be a need to change the information systems?

(d) Which IFRSs will affect the entity?

(e) Is this an opportunity to improve the accounting systems?

Once the initial evaluation of the current position has been made, the entity can determine the nature of any assistance required.

Other considerations

- Will the change affect debt covenants and other legal contracts?

- Is there any affect on performance related pay?

- Any changes in reporting should be communicated to analysts

Harmonisation of IFRS

There are a number of reasons why the harmonisation of accounting standards would be beneficial. Businesses operate on a global scale and investors make investment decisions on a worldwide basis. There is thus a need for financial information to be presented on a consistent basis. The advantages are as follows.

1 Multi-national entities

Multi-national entities would benefit from closer harmonisation for the following reasons.

- Access to international finance would be easier as financial information is more understandable if it is prepared on a consistent basis.

- In a business that operates in several countries, the preparation of financial information would be easier as it would all be prepared on the same basis.

- There would be greater efficiency in accounting departments.

- Consolidation of financial statements would be easier.

2 Investors

If investors wish to make decisions based on the worldwide availability of investments, then better comparisons between entities are required. Harmonisation assists this process, as financial information would be consistent between different entities from different regions.

3 International economic groupings

International economic groupings, e.g. the EU, could work more effectively if there were international harmonisation of accounting practices. Part of the function of international economic groupings is to make cross-border trade easier. Similar accounting regulations would improve access to capital markets and therefore help this process.

IASB relationship with national standard setters

The IASB has issued a draft memorandum that sets out how national and regional standards setters and the IASB should work together towards a single set of high quality, understandable and enforceable global accounting standards. The draft proposes that national and regional standard setter should:

- take prime responsibility for identifying and dealing with domestic regulatory barriers to adopting or converging with IFRS

- encourage nations to participate in international convergence efforts in their own regulatory field where this would facilitate financial reporting convergence.

The IASB should:

- ensure it makes relevant information available so that other standard setters can be fully informed of the IASB's activities and future plans

- maintain an up to date database of technical issues reported by other standard setters

- provide sufficient time to allow other standard setters to prepare additional material that would be required to place the IASB consultative documents in the national context to obtain input from local constituents.

Recent developments

The harmonisation process has gathered pace in the last few years. From 2005 all European listed entities were required to adopt IFRS in their group financial statements. Many other countries decided to follow a similar process and there are many countries who have now adopted IFRS or are in the process of doing so.

Many national standard setters are committed to a framework of accounting standards based on IFRS.

Convergence with US GAAP

In October 2002, the IASB and the US standard setter the Financial Accounting Standards Board (FASB) announced the issuance of a memorandum of understanding ("Norwalk Agreement"), marking a step toward formalising their commitment to the convergence of U.S. and international accounting standards. This agreement was updated in February 2006.

The IASB are working on the short term convergence project as well as joint projects over the longer term.

- The scope of the **short-term convergence project** is limited to those differences between US GAAP and IFRS in which convergence around a high quality solution appears achievable in the short-term (by 2008). Because of the nature of the differences, it is expected that a solution can be achieved by choosing between existing US GAAP and IFRS.

Topics covered by this project include segment reporting (IFRS 8 issued November 2008), borrowing costs (amended IAS 23 issued March 2007) and revised IAS 27 and IFRS 3 (both issued January 2008).

- **Joint projects** are those that the standard setters have agreed to conduct simultaneously in a coordinated manner.

Joint projects involve the sharing of staff resources, and every effort is made to keep joint projects on a similar time schedule at each Board. Currently, the FASB and IASB are conducting joint projects to address financial statement presentation, business combinations, conceptual framework and revenue recognition.

- The IASB is currently undertaking a joint project with the US FASB to reduce the differences between IAS 12 and its US counterpart. The project is part of the short-term convergence project and a final standard expected in 2010.

- •The IASB published an ED on joint arrangements (joint ventures) in September 2007 and expects to release a final standard during 2009. This would adopt a substance over form approach and may also abolish proportional consolidation as a method of accounting for joint ventures.

- The IASB and FASB have chosen to defer completing projects on government grants and impairment until other work is complete.

 Exam focus

Adoption of IFRS may be less important than it was in the past as all listed entities in the European Union now publish their financial statements based upon application of IFRS. However, it is still an important topic as non-listed companies may choose to voluntarily adopt IFRS in place of national standards. As a result of the harmonisation process taking place between UK FRS (and national reporting standards elsewhere) and IFRS, the transition process to IFRS is not as tortuous as it may have been in earlier years.

Harmonisation of IFRS with US GAAP has been, and continues to be, an important driver in the development of IFRS. You should be aware that recently issued and amended standards (IAS 23, IAS 27, IFRS 3 and IFRS 8) are a result of this process. This process is continuing and includes work on financial instruments and revenue recognition, together with the development of a common conceptual framework.

Within EN-gage Complete Text Chapter 22, attempt TYU 1 Pailing.

Recent examination questions include:

- December 2001 - Nettle
- June 2008 – Transition to IFRS.

chapter 18

Current issues

In this chapter

- Overview.
- Recent developments.
- The move to comprehensive reporting of gains and losses (IAS 1 revised)

Issues

- Make sure you can discuss current issues on the basis of

  - the current accounting treatment

  - the proposed new accounting treatment

  - the reasons for introducing the new treatment

- Be able to **discuss** and **calculate** the effects of new standards / exposure drafts

Recent developments

- **Draft IFRS for SMEs**

  A draft IFRS for small and medium-sized entities was issued in January 2009. By removing choices for accounting treatment, eliminating topics that are not generally relevant to SMEs and simplifying methods for recognition and measurement, the resulting draft standard reduces the volume of accounting guidance applicable to SMEs by more than 85 per cent when compared with the full set of IFRSs. As a result, the exposure draft offers a workable, self-contained set of accounting standards that would allow investors for the first time to compare SMEs' financial performance across international boundaries on a like for like basis. Whilst this would be a further element of convergence between UK FRS and IFRS, there is no equivalent reporting standard within US GAAP.

- **Annual Improvements to Financial Reporting Standards**

  The IASB has adopted an annual procedure to deal with minor, non-urgent amendments to IAS and IFRS. The first annual improvements standard was issued in May 2008, and effective from 1 January 2009. This will be an annual process with a similar procedure adopted by the UK ASB.

- **Harmonisation of IAS with UK FRS**

  There has been an on-going process of harmonisation between IAS/IFRS and UK FRS. Many of the more recently issued UK FRS also incorporates harmonisation with IFRS as part of their drafting and approval process. This applies to UK FRS 21 (Events after the reporting date), UK FRS 22 (Earnings per share) UK FRS 23 (Accounting for foreign currency transactions) and reporting standards dealing with financial instruments for example. One point to note is that IFRS 8 Operating Segments has not yet been approved for application in the UK, and therefore UK SSAP 25 Segmental Reporting continues to apply.

- **Harmonisation of IAS with US GAAP**

  This process includes harmonisation of reporting standards, for example IFRS 3 Revised dealing with measurement of goodwill and NCI within group accounts, together with work to develop a conceptual framework acceptable to both IASB and the Financial Accounting Standards Board in the USA.

- **Management commentary**

  Publication of an ED is expected during 2009. The ED provides guidance on additional information to be disclosed in annual financial statements. It links the commentary directly to the financial statements. It also identifies essential content which should be included within the commentary.

- **Fair Value measurement**

  This project aims to develop a consistent approach and a single source of guidance for the measurement of items recognised in the financial statements,. A DP was issued in November 2005 by the IASB, followed by an ED in May 2009. It would not require the application of fair value accounting unless already required by a current IAS/IFRS. The ED is consistent with proposals issued in the US on this topic and is part of the long-term convergence project to harmonise IFRS and US GAAP.

- **Conceptual framework**

  There is a long-term joint project between the IASB and FASB to develop a common conceptual framework, based upon the existing framework used by both boards. The project comprises eight stages, the first four of which are currently active:

  – Objectives and qualitative characteristics, with an ED issued in May 2008. The key objective is to provide financial information which is relevant to providers of equity investors, lenders and other creditors. Two fundamental qualitative characteristics are identified (relevance and faithful representation) – together with additional enhancing characteristics (timeliness, understandability, comparability and verifiability).

  – Elements and recognition, which has the objective of revising and clarifying the definitions of assets and liabilities and to clarify criteria for recognition and derecognition.

  – Measurement, which has the objective of providing guidance to selection of measurement bases which satisfy the objectives and qualitative characteristics of financial reporting. This is likely to focus upon fair values, together with possible alternatives and exceptions.

- The reporting entity, this could be an individual company or a corporate group under common control.
- Presentation and disclosure
- Purpose and status
- Application to not-for-profit entities
- Remaining issues

Recent examination questions include:

- Pilot Paper – Q4 - transition to IFRS
- December 2007 – Q4 – harmonisation of a conceptual framework
- June 2008 – Q4 – consistency between UK and international accounting standards
- December 2008 – Q4 – costs and benefits of accounting standards.

Exam focus

Current issues will always be a key feature of section B of the examination, typically comprising a question requiring an essay-style answer. This could include questions which have a conceptual or theoretical focus, and therefore may draw upon your knowledge and understanding of the Framework. Be aware that the Examiner has indicated that this could also include a computational element. You should regularly review the ACCA web site for articles of current or topical interest relevant for paper P2.

Index

R

S

T

V